A Magnetic Conspiracy

A Magnetic Conspircy

By

Raymond Lee Hegstad

This is a work of fiction, names, characters, places, and incidents are the product of the author's imagination, or used factiously. Any resemblance to actual events or locales or persons, living or dead, is entirely coincidental or intentionally disguised.

A Magnetic Conspiracy

By

Raymond Lee Hegstad

Prolog

With surprising ease, the Exacto blade had cut through her young flesh. She had expected a trickle of blood, but it was now flowing as freely as ketchup from a ripped apart packet. She mused that most people would call it despair, but she would call it courageous resolve. Her illegitimate child had been taken from her and she had brought disgrace to the family name: there was also an element of revenge in her motive.

Hypnotically, she watched as the red elixir of life mixed with the water. For a brief moment it floated as a bold red, and then it began changing to weaker and weaker shades of pink. It was becoming frail, just like her life. In a sudden change of heart she panicked…she attempted to stand up. She fought to stabilize her feet on the slippery bottom of the tub, but she collapsed. With blinding speed, her head was hurdling toward the bathtub fixtures.

* * *

Inside the Pennsylvania bank the temperature was like the chill of a vegetable crisper. She put her fingers to her cold lips and blew on them. Even the tone coming from the telephone sounded cold. After the third chirp, she picked up the receiver: the plastic felt like frozen meat.

"I'm sorry, sir, but the bank manager is not yet in…we're not really open, sir. You see our furnace is barely working." She paused, but all she could hear was the heavy breathing of an angry man. "His car won't start, sir. May I take a message?" She tried to sound as experienced as she could, but she was only a young high school student who was part of a training program.

The voice grumbled and then said, "I want Mr. Coleridge to prepare twenty-five, one-thousand-dollar bills…put them in a small bank pouch. I will pick up the pouch toward the end of your business day. He knows me…we've done this before."

"And the name, sir;" Her numb fingers scratched out the information. "Buford, yes, <u>C</u>. Buford…I have it, sir." Her stiff fingers replaced the phone.

She was startled by a noise: the furnace repair man was knocking at the door, she waved at him…he was well known. *Heat at last.* Thinking it was a good time to take a break, she and her four co-workers went to the company break room…the coffee was hot. "Guess what?" She spent the next twenty minutes talking about her mysterious caller who wanted the twenty-five thousand dollars…and in cash.

The next day, the twenty-three year old Mr. C. Buford was found dead, a blunt force trauma wound to the back of his head. The local skating pond was the site of the mystery…thin ice was blamed.

The young girl wondered, *Could the twenty-five thousand dollars in cash have anything to do with the death of C. Buford?* The newspapers and the police had said nothing about finding any money…that made her wonder even more. It was her nature…she felt responsible…even guity.

Chapter 1

To Peterrr Manning, Fort Walton Beach, Florida was always muggy and, in summer, oppressively hot air that never moved, lingering on for months. Today the temperature was in the high 90s and the humidity hung around like a panting racetrack Greyhound.

Taking frequent showers only resulted in walking around with a fresh coat of sticky water. The beach provided some relief, but very little, as the ocean temperature at Fort Walton regularly ran in the mid 80s, hot enough to melt surfers' blue wax right off the board (.at least that was the joke at the local bars). Temporary relief was had from incoming big breakers that beat your body until you felt like a boxer's sparing partner. The brackish water left a sticky coating of salt on your sunburned carcass.

Carl and Betsey dashed in and out of the incoming waves, mixing bravery with shouts of childish delight "Are you sure they're safe…those waves look pretty big, Peterrr," Marissa Manning shouted in an accusatory pitch; a born worrier when it came to her children. You might say she was a full blown paranoid. "Peterrr oh, Peterrr…I think we should get them out of that water," jutting her chin at the sea-green breakers churning up white froth.

Marissa wasn't a striking beauty, but she had sharp features which could set her apart when she smiled—white teeth, noble nose, and piercing eyes. As a teenager she had been adopted by her uncle, an American

New England patrician family. If one looked closely, lines of cosmetic surgery were evident, the real pains she kept locked in her private thoughts.

"My God, Marissa! You never want the kids to have any fun. Carl will keep an eye on Betsey." Without turning around, Peterrr Manning jabbed the pole of their beach umbrella into the white crystalline sand coverering the beach. Stepping back to admire his placement of the pole and associated apparatai, he glanced at the kids. "See, they've already found some playmates…let them have some fun."

Peterrr turned about and, as if moved by intuition, squinted as he strained to study the two children.

Not wanting Marissa to see him looking, he knew her comments were not to be taken lightly and she seldom grew concerned without reason.

She noticed his concern and gave him her famous "evil eye," a glance which shot rays of familial disapproval. Knowing Peterrr had a very thin layer of self approval, she took a different approach, "Aren't there sharks out there?"

Peterrr tightened his lips and took a deep breath. He closed his eyes as he reached inside the large beach-cooler he had just lugged some thirty feet though boiling white sand. "If you're so worried, Marissa, go get them—" He knew she would not walk down to the edge of the water, or even yell at the children as Marissa Manning was never going to be labeled *the bad guy*…to the kids, their friends or anyone else. That was Peterrr's job.

"Well…I don't like it!" she said, her lips not showing it but the words accompanied by a distinctive invisible pout.

"Look, Marissa, we came down here to cool off and let the kids have some fun…not feed the damned sharks! Do you see any shark fins out there? Well, I don't either!" Peterrr took a deep swig from his bottle of Budweiser and placed the cold bottle against his forehead. He glanced again at the familiar looking man on the beach.

Not more than ten feet away, a young woman turned to Peterrr and Marissa, the woman's long brown hair flowing over her shoulder and cascading down her tanned back. Blue-rimmed sunglasses covered steel gray eyes. "Did you say *sharks?*" she said, the unmistakable tone clearly evident that mothers use when concerned about their children. "My children are over there they are…playing next to the water—"The woman continued to settle into her beach spot and mutter about beach safety all the while.

Marissa punched Peterrr in the leg. "Hey, see…she's worried too." Marissa raised her voice to address the stranger, "My husband just made a comment about sharks…not that there *are* sharks out here." She thought a moment, trying to recall the woman from memory, a person she might have known from years past, "Do I know you?"

"I don't think so— we're new to the area," she said as she spread out her beach blanket and moved her purse to the side.

After an understanding nod, but still thinking about it some, Marissa adjusted her sunglasses and turned to watch her children.

Ten minutes passed and Marissa couldn't help herself. She turned to the woman and said, "Are those your children playing with ours?"

"I'm Sara Buford…my husband, Chad, is there with our children." She pointed to the spot where four children, including the

Manning kids, were building a sand castle under the watchful eye of a young man. "Are those your children?" Sara flashed a smile and looked over the top rim of her glasses.

Peterrr nodded as he took another belt from his cold beer.

Marissa's insides churned but she responded with a polite, "Yes…Carl's nine and Betsey's seven…going on seventeen." She followed with a flash of her wintry-white teeth, "They seem to be having fun." Without pause she announced, "I'm Marissa…and this is Peterrr," she gave a head-pointing gesture, "the one guzzling the beer." This time she made a more thorough examination of their new beach neighbor.

"Chad wanted to bring some beer but all we had was bottled and they don't allow glass on the beach." Sarah glanced up at Peterrr's glass bottle of beer and muttered, "Oops…."Her hand covered an impish smile.

Examining his bottle with only a casual concern, Peterrr grinned, "I didn't know that." He looked down at Marissa, "Did you?" Without waiting for an answer, he said, "I'd be glad to get your husband in trouble by offering him one of mine." He released a muffled belly laugh and looked around as he slyly slipped a cold bottle under his bare arm. "Wow, that's cold!"

"I think he would enjoy one of your contraband," Sarah said, musing at her creative use of words. She went on, "Mr…?"

Changing to an Australian accent, he said, "Peterrr Manning at your service, Mum." He picked up a Mickey Mouse beach towel and covered up the beer in question then said, "I'm gonna check on the kids." He gave Marissa a brief glance, "…I'll be back with an accurate shark count!" As he walked by Sarah he looked down at her and admired her sensuous figure, "Chad, you say, Mum?"

"Yes…Chad. The children are Warren, eleven, and Glenda, nine." She laughed and turned her attention to Marissa. "Mind if I join you…I have a feeling we're going to be deserted for a while." Sarah got up and moved closer to Marissa.

In a tense gesture, Marissa adjusted her sunglasses, "Sure…I'd like some company." Instinctively, she evaluated the woman's clothing, accessories and figure and couldn't decide if she approved of all three—but that would have to keep for now. It was Sarah's husband that interested Marissa.

Having reintroduced herself, Sarah wiggled her butt into the blanket covered sand. "Sooo, what brings you to Florida, Marissa? I must say, your name sounds familiar—"

"First name or last?" Marissa said, flashing though a plethora of reasons, some true, some less than true. "We've been stationed at Eglin…Washington DC before that. Peterrr comes from a long line of cops." She smiled, "How about you…Sarah?"

Still focused on her question to Marissa, she skewed her jaw but answered only with, "Oh, nothing…I think there was a Marissa at my high school, not a common name back then. A sophomore or junior, I think…that's all." *Marissa DeVunder,* Sarah thought to herself.

"Oh…imagine that. Well, I was born in Switzerland, but my parents were Americans living overseas." The tone of Marissa's answer left little doubt ,but what she considered that line of conversation closed…and closed it was.

Chapter 2

Her tiny hand shaded her eyes from the late morning sun, "Dad, there's a man coming" Glenda Buford put the finishing touches on the seaside parapet and turned about to run into the pounding surf. Warren, pretending to be a ravenous sea monster, chased his sister as she attempted to escape the monster's fiendish claws.

Inspired by Warren's example, Carl and Betsey Manning jumped to their feet. Carl shouted as he broke into a full sprint into the sea foam, "That's our father, mister." Little Carl jerked his sister's arm as he raced past her, resulting in her head hitting first into the edge of wet sand. She came up crying and pursued Carl like a darting barracuda.

Chad turned his attention to the approaching man who stood about six feet tall with stringy short hair, a trifle overweight. Without telling his wife, Chad had come to the beach with the specific intent of meeting the Mannings. Three days earlier he had come across their files.

Chad held up his hand and made the universal finger-split made famous by Star Trek's Mr. Spock. He sported a broad, thin-lipped grin.

"I come in peace?" Quickly, Peterrr yelled, "One of these days Betsey is going to flatten you, boy." The handshake came next."Peterrr Manning here."

Chad put out his hand, "I'm Chad Buford. How are the girls getting along?" Under the shade of the beach umbrella and distance from the water, the features of Marissa and Sarah were blurred.

Peterrr glanced toward the umbrella to find two ladies deep in conversation…   "I'd say…they're checking each other out." He nodded toward the quartet of children who were being knocked over by the frothy green surf. "Those two are ours," he said, pointing. He shook his head and laughed, "Quite a handful."

"So are ours;" *Meeting Peterrr Manning was easy. I wonder how meeting his wife will go.*

In silence, the two men watched the children play. Like fledgling sea otters, the kids moved about in the water as they struggled to stand up against each charging wave. Quickly, the two boys separated from the girls and began exploring the sea bottom, replete with tiny crabs, snails and colored rocks that looked like pieces of candy.

"Are you from here?" Chad asked, as he kept watching the kids. The words rolled out of his mouth as casually as if asking for the time of day.

Peterrr hesitated, "I think you know that answer, major…we've been expecting you." Peterrr Manning offered a wry grin.

"Yep, I'm an American, but my grandparents were from Australia. Every so often we visit the grand folks on the Island…I can slip into Aussie as easy as pie."

Peterrr smiled and cleared his throat, then he thickened his accent. "Yeah, I get that quite a bit…I get a bit disappointed if no one asks." He reached inside of the beach towel he was carrying. "Almost forgot…brought you something." As he handed the towel to Chad he added, "I'm rather proud of me Aussie heritage, don't mind sayin'. Hope you like Bud…can't get a decent lager here, Mate."

Without comment, Chad glanced around, as if expecting the Coast Guard to haul him off under the pretext of breaking beach etiquette. "God, could I use a beer…thanks." Making a show of covering his head from the sun, he took a quick guzzle from the slippery wet bottle of Bud. From under the beach towel he said, "Sarah…you met Sarah?"

"Yeah, lovely lady, Mate." Peterrr continued pouring on his Australian bit—it made him feel manly and something superior to the common bloke. He also could do accents in German, Russian and several other languages…but while in Florida, Peterrr avoiding doing an excellent Cuban variation.

Chad snickered and continued, "Sarah had a fit when I wanted to bring some beer to the beach. Bottles aren't allowed…'fraid of the glass I guess."

"She told Marissa the same thing. Blooming shame when a man can't even have a beer at a lovely spot like this."

The two men bantered back and forth for the better part of twenty minutes, then the children, by now, slowed down to dragging tired legs through the saltwater.

The rant was still going on when Chad shrugged and put his hand on Peterrr's arm. "Out there…" Chad's thoughts were interrupted as he focused on the children and spoke in a soft tone."…Let's get the kids out of the water, Peterr, like now."

Peterrr Manning saw what had caused Chad's hushed tone. Not more than fifty yards past the children, a set of small dorsal fins cruised the water. Quickly, the men dashed to the water's edge, the boys and girls still separated. Chad became oblivious to the Manning children, as it was Warren and Glenda who mattered. But it was Carl Manning and Chad's son, Warren, closest to where he went into the water.

There wasn't time to discuss the situation, as the sharks began to change course to circle their prey. Chad agonized over the situation but didn't have long to make any judgments about Peterrr…aside from his file. He didn't know what kind of person Peterrr Manning was and couldn't predict what he would do. Behind him, far off to the beach umbrella, he could hear Sarah and Marissa shouting.

"Shark…shark!" the beach crowd began yelling. It was like the ending scene from the movie, *The Body Snatchers.*

As if in slow motion, Peterrr Manning glanced to his left in time to see Chad grab Carl and Warren, cradling one under each arm. Across the chasm that lay between them, the eyes of the two men met and an invisible exchange took place. *Thanks for getting my son…I've got your little girl.* Peterrr Manning gripped Glenda by the back of her halter top and grabbed Betsey under her flailing arms…her small life vest made it difficult to carry her close to his body.

Both men knew that the easy part was over—getting the kids to safety without losing a leg or becoming shark chum was going to be somewhat harder.

By this time, the women were at the water's edge, Marissa was about to run into the shallow white water but Sarah grabbed her so hard that she ended up hitting the wet sand on her behind as the incoming foam threw a mini-wall of water and knocked off her sunglasses.

"Get your hands off of me!" Marissa struggled to get to her feet, at the same time taking a swipe at Sarah's legs.

Sarah put a hand on Marissa's shoulder and held her down. As she tried to talk some sense into her, she said, "The men have got the kids, Marissa… For chrissake! Don't give the sharks another target!"

"Mind your own goddamn business, lady!" Marissa said, breaking free of Sarah and running up the beach, wiping at her open mouth and sputtering and cursing.

Peterrr and Chad could see the sharks were small, probably no more than three or four feet long, but they were in extremely shallow water and they stirred up the ocean bottom as their tails swept from side to side. They slowed down as they moved between the men carrying the squirming children and the dry sand of the beach.

With as much haste as possible, the men made way to the beach and dry land, but they also instinctively moved closer together so the sharks could not pick them off individually. Soon they were in single file and moving as if they were one larger prey…a less inviting target.

The water was only a bit more than two feet deep when the pair of killers passed next to Chad's legs and he felt a nudge as the second shark bumped his ankle.

Looking down, through the murky sediment, he could see a thin trail of red beginning to form. "He clipped me!" Chad yelled. "I'm bleeding...run for the beach, Peterr."

But Chad was thinking about Glenda who was trailing behind the tall, somewhat overweight man. He might reach land, but Glenda was trailing behind him as if she were a piece of bait on a fishing lure.

"I'm coming!" His Australian accent was gone. Peterrr's heavy legs churned the water and pounded prints into the sandy bottom as he moved behind Chad Buford. Conscious of the few people who were now lining the beach, he focused on the worried face of Marissa who looked more angry than anxious. His heart was pounding, more from fear than from effort. Considered by some as a selfish man, Peterrr wondered if he was afraid for himself or for the children, thoughts one might think in a time like this.

Sarah waited until Chad had reached water no more than a foot deep before she rushed forward to get Warren from under his arm. Frantically, she checked Warren's body then hugged him while he sniffled and looked about in confusion. She watched as Carl ran to his mother.

Chad moved to Peterrr and snatched Glenda out of the water just as a shark made a pass as, otherwise, she would have most probably had to live the rest of her life minus some toes. She was now safely on dry land, with only a nick…just like her father.

Marissa reacted by beating Peterrr about the chest, which he knew was her way of dealing with the fear. But with each child firmly gripping his large legs, Peterrr put his arms around Marissa and pulled her tightly to his hairy chest. "There were two."

She melted until she slid down his wet body and caressed the children.

"The count was two, Dear…*two* sharks." For Peterrr, it was just another day with his emotional wife. He looked down at the top of her head, her hair was thick and black…so opposite to the white-sandy beach. When he looked up, he saw a lifeguard tending to Chad's ankle and Glenda's right toe.

Chad's eyes moved from the blanket that had been spread for him and Glenda. In spite of Glenda's injury, he felt Peterrr had done a good job of rescuing his precious one…it was doubtful he could have gotten to Warren and Glenda in time to save them both.

Sarah was kneeling to the side, comforting Glenda.

Making sure his glance stayed unnoticed, Chad looked to Marissa Manning, *Marissa… Manning…huh?*

Sarah did her own silent snooping at Marissa…*Heather's mysterious cousin, huh?"*

Chapter 3

It was as if the shark incident had never happened. Chad and Sarah Buford stopped at a local McDonalds but Glenda's foot was too sore to do any playing in the fun zone. Warren slurped his chocolate shake and scattered his French fries about the table. As usual, he began building a small log cabin. An unwritten truce had been formed—if they didn't talk about it…it never happened. For a while, shark talk was taboo—so too was the subject of Marissa Manning.

Leaning across the Formica-topped table, Chad rested his elbows on the surface and examined his hamburger as he talked to Sarah. "So…what did you and Mrs. Manning talk about?" He was probing.

Sarah glanced at Glenda and whispered, "Before or after the sharks?" She dipped her head in the direction of their daughter.

Before—" He took a big bite and continued his detailed examination of the Big Mac.

"Just girl stuff…nothing specific. I doubt she remembers me…the inquiry was a long time ago, and she was still in Europe." Sarah reached into her pile of condiments and opened another packet of ketchup for Warren, as he was using it for calking on his log cabin. "She asked what brought us here, but I never got around to answering her question." She paused, "You know, I know what to say, Chad, but he's with the APs or CID…it think." There was a distinct edge to her voice. Narrowing her eyes, she continued in a hush, "Lord knows you've made such a big thing about it… Well, I just don't see what all the fuss is about."

With a slow shake of his head, he spoke through a mouth full of burger, "Okay, Sarah…you did a good job. I'm sorry…

It's just that I will probably be working with Peterrr Manning. In this case, he was expecting our arrival. He says that Blain told him we were coming."

"Daddy, you talked with your mouth full. Mommy says that is…is impolite." Glenda's legs were too short to carry her feet to the floor and she swung the uninjured foot to and fro as she colored in her placemat. At present, she was enjoying a mild sedative that dulled the pain from the surgical stitching and the drug made her words sound a bit slurred.

"Mommy's right, Pumpkin… Sorry." In spite of himself, Chad smiled and a few tears rolled down his cheeks. His heart skipped as he took a deep breath—if that shark had been just a little faster, it might have grabbed her by the ankle and taken her out to sea.The thought of her not sitting there with her little legs swinging and her treble voice talking to him was just too much to bear. At that moment he realized he should just sit and listen to her talk…forever, if she were willing to do that. He was thankful that no one asked him why he was tearing up.

Sara sucked in her lips and pretended she was not noticing the way Chad was wiping his cheeks with the back of his hands…she loved him. *God, he is such a chameleon— tough as garnet and soft as melting ice cream.* He was a passionate man, but not one of those emotional men who fell apart at the slightest offense or hint of a crisis. Even his love making was put forth with the intensity of a jungle cat, yet the gentleness of a purring baby kitten—an absolute enigma.

 "I suppose we'll have to have the Mannings over for a few brews." Chad started collecting the table trash as if he had not said a word. "Let's go, guys." Moving to the other side of the table, he picked up Glenda and gave her a peck on the cheek. With his left hand he grabbed Warren's ketchup-coated fingers…and gave Sarah a proud smile as he kissed her salty lips. "Good fries, huh?" Scooping Warren's soggy fry-house, "Sorry, Son, can't take it home or have it bronzed."

 Warren pretended to be hurt, "Oh, gee, Dad." He was small for his age, just a late bloomer they told him. Warren enjoyed "milking" his size as an excuse to get by with small-kid stuff.

Heavy cumulous clouds, gray and foreboding, were moving west and beginning to deposit a late afternoon monsoon as the family raced to the car to avoid getting drenched any further. Like bouncing teardrops, the rain began to dance over the warm, black asphalt, causing little puffs of fog. It would be a good day to just stay at home and cuddle up on the couch…maybe with the kids—they could just hug each other. Sarah hoped Chad would not have to go to Eglin tonight…but he probably would. The question of *inviting the Manning's over for a brew* was postponed.

"Working tonight?" She struggled to not let one scintilla of accusation color her tone, but she was pretty sure a tinge of disappointment seeped through.

No doubt it was tough for Sarah, but she really was a good trooper…she knew the score and seldom complained. She and Chad had renewed their relationship when she served under him, a romance that went on "undetected" by the military for the three years she was on active duty. Tonight Chad was going to Duke Field, twelve miles north of the East Gate on Highway 85. The 919th Special Operations Wing (AFRES) and the 728th Tactical Control Squadron were there. Chad had managed to obtain a job as a non-military security advisor to the AAC (Air Armament Center). For identification purposes he was allowed to use his reserve rank of Major. Most people who knew the Bufords would have assumed their income was from a small inheritance or a lucrative multi-level marketing business.

"I won't be gone long, Hon, just going to Field Three to see how the paperwork is doing." Quickly he changed the subject, "I'll kiss the kids goodnight…and don't forget Glenda has a follow up appointment at the hospital." Chad could tell something was bothering Sarah but had a sense that now might not be the best time to press her for any details. "Get some rest, Hon…"

The kids were in the other room playing: Warren had insisted they play shark…of course he was the prehistoric attacker. Any other time, the yells and screams would have been offensive, but tonight it was a celestial concert for reasons obvious.

"Sure…just a bit worn out." Using her long fingers, she brushed back her hair from her forehead. Looking into Chad's eyes she could see his love for her, and it made her want to cry. "Tomorrow will be better, Major." She saluted him and winked. She couldn't help thinking he had looked just as handsome twenty years ago when they first met…but she seldom allowed that time in her life to resurface. Local legend had it that Marissa's cousin, Heather, had somehow been involved in the Buford drowning accident. Chad never thought the death was an accident, but murder for money or his philandering…or both? Then again, he was willing to concede that he could be wrong.

Chapter 4

With the children safely tucked away for the night, Sarah pulled a bottle of white wine from the family's custom built, wall refrigerator. Situated behind a false book shelf concealing an inner glass door, it could hold forty-eight bottles of chilled wine— twenty-four bottles of white wine in the lower hold…and in the upper portion twenty-four bottles of red wine and kept at a proper fifty-five degrees Fahrenheit.

It had not just been a taxing day—it had been a horrible day. A part of her past had suddenly jumped out at her and violated the security she had felt for years. For a second, she rested the cold thin wine glass against her lower lip. She fought against an involuntary shudder as she gulped down half the glass—a feeling of depression was jumping about in her brain, trying to find a place to settle. Chad had sensed her uneasiness, and she finished the rest of the glass and poured another. It wasn't a question of whether she should confide in Chad or not, as he was too smart and could get investigation files that other people could not. She felt confident even if he chose to dig, he would never find her secret in a file folder, let alone on the Internet…it was securely locked in her vault of memories.

At seven minutes after midnight, her cell phone rang. The phone was buried in her purse, so the sound would not disturb Warren and Glenda. "Hello?" She assumed it was Chad, just checking in.

"How're you doing?" The voice was hushed…like someone not wanting to be overheard.

Sarah brought her glass to her face and rested it against her cheek. She was certain she did not know the person behind the voice, but this would be the second time she had received one of these strange calls. The call was intended to bring out memories she had struggled to forget and she desperately wanted the voice to go away, for good.

She downed the glass of wine, her fourth, and hoped the wine would give her some courage or at least dull her guilt. She snarled, "Go to hell!"

Quickly she punched the button on the top of her cell phone. It was now off.

Next, she picked up the receiver on her land-line and dropped it under a cushion on the over-stuffed chair. Her thinking had now turned to panic. For a moment, she pretended nothing happened…and the past would remain as buried as a Pharaoh's tomb. She poured another glass of white wine and began looking about the room; she was searching for something.

Her eyes stopped when they found her husband's collection of World War II

German Lugers. Mounted on the wall in their living room were eight of them, arranged to form a Nazi swastika. For what seemed like hours, she just stared at the wall and made believe she were listening to the jets take off from the air field. Her mind was trapped in a recycling of repressed images quickly turning to peace-eating villains.

A hard knock on the front door caused Sarah to jump and she spilled a few drops of white wine on her lavender bed dress. She got up, brushing the offending spots as she approached the front door, then a quick glance at the wall clock…4:00 a.m. For a moment, she hesitated, fearing what might be on the other side. Looking through the peep hole, she could see the flashing lights of a Fort Walton Beach patrol car…

Slowly, she opened her front door, the mesh, outside steel security door firmly in place. "Yes, officer, can I help you?" She forgot about the glass of wine in her hand.

The officer looked back at his female partner who was observing from behind the steering wheel. "Ma'am, your husband, Major Buford, asked us to check on you. He said your phones were off, that it was unusual." He attempted to look over her shoulder and through the opening of the door jam. He lowered his voice to a barely audible tone, "If you are in need of assistance…please blink three times and we will leave and send in a special team."

She smiled and tipped her head to one side. Standing back from the door so the officer could see into the room, she quipped, "Just got a crank call, officer, nothing serious…you may tell my husband I will call him in a few minutes." She gave a chagrined look at her glass."Oops,"she said.She leaned forward and spoke in a confidential whisper, "I'll need some time to push a few buttons and get my phones working."

She again flashed her glass of wine, the amber liquid sloshing about like a trapped wave, "Thank you Mr. Officer…and Ms. Officer out there." She waved at the female officer in the car. "Have a pleasant night."

She closed the door and began to whimper like a wounded puppy. She wanted her life back…who was calling her? She didn't have a clue but suspected one day the murderer would feel the need to catch up with her—in person.

After calling Chad and assuring him she
had taken the phones off of the hook
because of some crank calls from teenagers,
she checked on the children…still sound
asleep. She then turned off all house lights
and checked outside…nothing. Her years of
working with the Military Police were
coming in handy—it had been a happy time
and, as a lieutenant, she had worked together
with Chad on a personal level.

One hour after the local police had left; she
received the customary follow-up call to
make sure she was alright. She smiled as
she walked through the standard routine
with the desk officer assigned to the job.
Now, she was flipping through a shoebox
full of papers and newspaper articles, the
trail of her past. The papers were concerned
with the mysterious but apparently
accidental drowning death of a twenty-three
year old college student and the ensuing
investigation. As in the past, the papers
received teardrops causing the paper to turn
the flat surface into little bumps, like a child
with hives. She was doing her best to decide
what to do but how could she explain to

Chad what might have really happened at the pond?

The phone rang…her stomach tightened and her heart began to race, Sarah's face becoming a dark pink as the blood attempted to supply a frightened and confused mind. Every time Sarah poured through her secret shoebox she wondered if Chad knew about the past which followed her like an avenging cherub. He was a professional, and a good one, it was almost inconceivable he did not know, but she could not find the courage to confront him.

The phone was still ringing, she picked it up—

"Just following up, Honey, are you all right?" Chad sounded concerned, but not frightened for her safety. "What took you so long to answer?"

She laughed, "You know how it is…go to the bathroom and someone is bound to call. Sorry, Hon, it…it's been one of those nights, but the kids have slept through all of it." Her eyes were moving around as she struggled to think of something else to say. "When will you be home?" She was glad when he didn't ask any more questions.

A brief silence followed, "Err, that's why I called. Something has come up and it looks like I'm going to be stuck here a couple more hours." He weighed the silence that had taken over the phone line "I'm sorry, but I don't know how to get out of it. I was especially concerned when you turned off the phones…are you sure you're all right? Was the beach drama a bit much? Should I send one of the AP guys to keep an eye on the house?" He nodded to several personnel standing next to him. They had files and discs for his review.

Sarah sighed and ignored the questions, "Hey, it's okay… It's just that I didn't want to listen to a bunch of teenage pranksters for the rest of the night." She wanted to ask him to put a trace on the call she had received but didn't want to get him further involved in the problem. It was best for the family he did not have his hands in this mess. "I'll see you in the morning… Don't worry about it. We'll be fine…the kids are sleeping."

Chad was troubled because he knew she would not want to bother him with "the little things." After all, she was a tough lady…when she needed to be. He hoped this was not one of those occasions. "Okay, but…if you need help, call me. If I'm not immediately available, call the base police or locals. I might be out of touch for a while, but I want you to not try to be the tough guy…okay."

"Sure…" Her brain screamed to tell him everything and clear the air, even get his help, but instead she calmed her voice and infused her words with a sexual tone, "See you in the morning, Sailor…I hope you're ready for me."

Despite himself, he blushed and smiled, "Sure thing, Doll, bye."
He turned his outward attention to those waiting for him, but his mind was racing ahead. They had both been rocked by the realization that Marissa Manning was once Marissa DeVunder, cousin to the deceased Heather DeVunder. Up until the death of Charles Buford, Heather had been Charles' girlfriend. More than that… Then Sara's phone rang *It must be Chad* and she said, "Forget to tell me something, Sailor?"

A garbled voice began speaking. It was obvious the speaker was using an electronic scrambler."Who's Sailor?" the voice said. "…I just called to remind you… you have two lovely children.I'm sure you would miss them should anything, how shall I say it…happen. The past is the past…forget it. Leave it alone—" The gravely voice paused then became a hush; "You know what happens to prying people, don't you? Just ask your father…Oh, oh…That's right, you can't. He's dead."

Chapter 5

Glenda picked up her empty cereal bowl and dumped the remaining milk into the kitchen sink. "Mom…why were the police here? Did they come to visit Dad?" Chad's new job involved extended contacts and the local police had begun checking in with him, but usually only by phone.

Excitedly, Warren asked, "Did they want to know about the sharks?"

Sarah smiled and ruffled Warren's bed-head hair then spoke in a very matter of fact tone, "No, Honey, they came here to check on us." She frowned at the spilled milk in the sink, "Some idiot called our house and started talking bad stuff, so I just took the phones off the hook…for a little while."

"You're not supposed to call people 'idiots,' Mom." Warren Buford was absent mindedly examining the writing on a box of Captain Crunch cereal; his eyes never leaving the box as he admonished his mother for her choice of words.

Sarah grinned and stepped behind Warren. Affectionately, she grabbed him by the shoulder and whispered in his ear, "What IDIOT said that?" She went away giggling with self-satisfaction.

Warren turned the box, "MOM!" He looked up from the box. "Betsey said so. She's not allowed to use that word."

"Betsey Manning?" Sarah could not think of a time, other than at the beach, when the children had been together. "She told you that when you were at the beach?"

He dropped his shoulders and rolled his eyes, "Daaa!" He took a deep breath and said, "At school, Mom…she rides the same bus…so does Carl."

"You didn't know that, Mom?" Glenda queried.

After grabbing the kids' empty lunch pails, she stopped and thought about the question. This was the first time she had even thought about it. "So…when you were at the beach, you already knew them?"

"We're the new kids, Mom. We had seen them, but we didn't know them… I think Dad knew their dad." Glenda pulled alongside her mother and started filling the lunch boxes.

Sarah felt confused and frowned, "What makes you think they knew each other?" She struggled to remain calm. He hadn't mentioned anything about knowing Peterrr Manning…or Marissa Manning, for that matter.

Glenda turned to make a face at her brother…she knew he wanted to interject his opinion. "I *didn't* say they *knew* each other, Mom…it's just that Dad seemed to know *who* Mr. Manning was. I figured it was because of Dad's work."

Getting up from his stool, Warren walked over to his mother and put his arm around her. "What's bothering you, Mom?" He was known for his insightfulness, but sometimes it bordered on being spooky.

Sarah smacked her lips and cupped his face between her hands, "You know how nosey we women are." She kissed his forehead, "I'll ask your father when he gets up…he had a rough night last night….he should be up soon." She handed Warren his lunch box, "Now, off with you, before you two miss the bus."

The children were not even out of the door before she began wondering what was going on. Why hadn't Chad mentioned he knew something about the Mannings? She would have loved to think it was probably that damned job of his, but it could be something else. So much secrecy—she understood the need for the secrecy, but that did not stop her from hating it.
Her mind then switched to last night and the phone calls. She needed to talk to someone, but Chad might not be up for another four hours. She had secrets herself…not many of them, but only the one that she could never find the strength to tell her husband. Sarah had wanted to ask Chad to tell her everything he knew about her past, but what if he didn't know anything…she didn't want to spark any curiosity which might result in digging

further. Her worry-wart mind was shocked back to reality when the phone rang. "Hello," involuntarily, Sarah's stomach clutched.

"Sarah?" the voice hesitated then continued, "Marissa Manning here. I just got the kids out of the house… Are yours gone?" She didn't wait for an answer, "How would you like a visit? Honestly, I just have to talk to someone who is taller than forty inches or a husband who is not a predatory male." At last there was a real break in the conversation. "Well? What about early brunch? I could meet you in an hour or so…?"

Sarah was not sure if it was her turn to say something as she was still recovering from the surprise call. "Ah…yeah, guess I could meet you…got some place in mind?"

"I was thinking the base officers' club…they've got great food and no one will be there this time of day. If it's like most O-Clubs, we'll practically have the place to ourselves." Marissa Manning spoke like a machine gun, her words seeming to melt into one long word needing to be separated and decoded.

"Oh, there will be people there, Marissa…there are always people at base clubs." Sarah hesitated and asked herself, *Are the Mannings military or civilians with base privileges?* Sarah's psychiatrist had told her this day would probably come. She reflected on the psychiatrist's words, *that which you dread may one day come to pass.* Sarah made a note to herself—to do a little research into Marissa Manning.

"I really must confess, I have something I need to discuss with you and I think you will want to chat about it." Her new tone now was now conspicuous.

Immediately, Sarah's mind flashed back to the annoying phone calls she had received the other night. Maybe Marissa knew something about the calls. "Well, the 'O Club' can be interesting." *Had Chad talked to her? Maybe I will be able to get some answers.* "Sure…I'll meet you there, just remember to dress casual."

"I hate playing dress-up, so no problem for me. See you there." The line clicked then hummed.

Without focusing on what was bothering her, she could feel a cloak of uneasiness settling in. Sarah had not thought about it, but why would Marissa ask a new person in town, a"civilian" at that, to go to the base for some rest and relaxation talk. For that matter, how was Marissa planning to get on base in the first place? She looked into the mirror as she put on the finishing cosmetic touches.

"She must know someone at the base." She turned from side to side to make sure her khaki Chinos were acceptable. Returning to the phone, she pressed *69 and got Marissa's phone number. She punched in the numbers and the phone retuned with an answering message… Apparently Marissa was not picking up or she had already left for the O-Club.

Quietly, Marissa left the house…certain Chad had slept through all of the phone chatter. She was equally certain he would not read the message she had left him—it was one of his bad habits.

The sticker on her car window identified the vehicle as authorized to enter Eglin Air Force Base, but Sarah needed to present her personal ID before passing through the gate. As she approached the guard, she smiled…the man had transferred in just before Chad and they had talked previously. "Good morning, Sergeant. How's Emily?"

"Just fine, Mrs. Buford…I'll tell her you asked. We're all glad the Major accepted the job, Ma'am." He gave her a crisp but unnecessary salute…she was now a civilian, but he had known her when she was an officer serving with Chad. "Are you visiting the Major, Ma'am?"

"No, just meeting one of the ladies for an early brunch." She thought for a second then said, "Did Mrs. Manning come by here?" It was a long shot, but Sarah had been a professional investigator and long ago had learned it never hurts to play a hunch."

"Captain Manning passed through not more than ten minutes ago, Ma'am, headed for, I believe, the O-Club."

"Thank you, Sergeant." She slipped the car into Drive and waited for the metal arm to rise and allow her passage onto the military base. *Well, well, well, so little rich girl, Marissa, is Military… So what the hell is she up to?* Sarah recalled her son, Warren, had said he thought his Dad knew something about Peterrr Manning, but Chad had not said one word to Sarah about knowing him. *Go figure!* Her impulse was to turn the car around and go back home but her curiosity was far too powerful to do such a thing.

Marissa chose a spot away from the lines of traffic which would soon arrive, and only four other vehicles were actually at the club. Upon entering the building, she wrinkled her nose as she became immediately aware of the stale, smoky smell and hundreds of different stages of decaying alcohol. Bacon and powdered eggs diluted the otherwise nasty odors. Meeting with Sarah had been her own idea—a bold move but was unlikely anyone would consider the meeting place as anything but normal. Marissa waved as Sarah's silhouette appeared in the doorway. Sarah was outlined by blazing sunlight shooting into the room like flames from an ascending rocket. The light disappeared as the door behind her closed.

With a friendly smile, Sarah approached the table. As she hefted her purse to a nearby chair, she sighed and said, "I never get used to the smell in these places, and the darkness...it's like a bat cave."

She took her chair to the right of Marissa, noticing she was in civilian clothes. "Have any trouble finding the place?" Sarah said lightly.

Sarah avoided eye contact. An innocent enough question, but if Marissa was a "Spook" she would know straightway it was a probative inquiry, but so what... Sarah chose to hide her knowledge about the Mannings…after all; Marissa had not mentioned they were military.

"The guard at the gate gave me good directions…no trouble at all." Marissa flashed a plastic smile and then reached out a friendly hand that fell gently on Sarah's forearm. "And you?"

"Piece of cake."

Chapter 6

Chad Buford had difficulty concentrating on the computer screen. For the last hour he had been looking over incoming FBI information, routine background examinations and follow-ups. His thinking centered on his concern for Sarah and the kids, the phone calls and the way Sarah had reacted. He pushed himself back from his desk and picked up his cup of cold coffee.

After scowling, he glanced at his watch and said, "Carla…I think I need a break. These reports are all starting to look alike—"

His overweight secretary set aside her latest pastry treat and mumbled, "Knock yourself out, boss…you just got here, but what the hell…who's counting?" She reached to one side and grabbed some paper for the high-speed HP Laser, "If you see one of those supply guys, tell them I'm running out of paper and to bring five boxes."

They both knew he would not be rushing over to the supply sergeant and ordering paper, but it was her way of calling attention to *small gripes*. "Sure thing, Carla, I'll be back in a couple of hours." He had a hunch he should zip home, grab lunch, and check on Sarah and the house, as the kids would be well settled at school. He had just missed them, and Sarah had probably gone out shopping. He grabbed his *spy kit* and pushed his chair into place at his desk.

"Going to check on something, Major?" She tipped her head as her eyes fell on his carry-all. It contained all sorts of bugging and debugging devices, not to mention a few questionable chemicals.

He patted the black kit which looked like nothing more than a large sample case used by a medical salesman. "Well, you never know, Carla, just routine."

Reading his mind, she said, "Why don't you check on home base…I mean, after all that ruckus the other night." She shifted her eyebrows as she referenced the strange phone calls. "Did anyone *clear* the place before you moved in?"

One of the reasons Chad put up with her sauce was, Carla was almost psychic when it came to certain things as well as experienced in espionage. As if the idea had never occurred to him, he replied, "Come to think of it, Carla… You know, I think that's a good idea— I don't think it was ever checked out. I'll be at home…in case someone needs me." He wrinkled his forehead as if deep in thought then made his way out of his corner office, northwest end, of one of the converted airplane hangers, the coolest and least humid spot in the building…so they told him.

Using a back road off the base, he considered calling Sarah and letting her know he was coming, but he also knew she was feeling rather jumpy about the telephone; besides, she liked it when he just "popped in" unannounced.

Chad had not expected to find the driveway empty, and this naturally set off his mind's alarm clock. He checked on the positioning of his shoulder pistol. After a quick glace around the periphery, he moved to the back door and set down his black case. He tried the door handle—it was locked. That was good. Maybe she had just gone shopping. He fumbled through his keys, found the right one and unlocked the door... Cautiously, he entered the house, prepared for any eventually.

In five minutes, he had checked every room and closet, viewed the yard from all inside windows and preliminarily *cleared* the house. He then put on his latex gloves, a routine procedure so automatic as to be called compulsive.

His heart started to pound as he picked up the phone and pressed the REDIAL button.

"Hello... You have reached the home of Mr. and Mrs. Manning. We are not available to take your call at this time... Please leave your name, phone number, and

a brief message and we will return your call
as soon as possible. Thank you." Then
came the log of incoming/outgoing calls…

He replaced the phone on the hook and sat
down on one of their bar stools. This was
unexpected…Why had Sarah called
Marissa; to talk about the kids, the sharks,
or maybe the good ol' days in Pittsburg,
Pennsylvania? A chilling tingle passed
through his gut. Is that why Sarah wasn't
home? One by one the questions popped
into his head, all of them leading to other
questions and raising his concern. Should
he ask Sarah about it, or would she consider
it more meddling in her business?
He went to the refrigerator and plucked out a
bottle of beer, twisted off the cap and began
to nurse the cold bottle. He glanced at his
spy box and made a decision—he would
scan the house again, this time thoroughly,
while he made up his mind.

The equipment Major Chad Buford used
was two notches above what the FBI used—
he always was made privy to the CIA Black
Ops Department field equipment, considered
some of the best acoustic and signal tracers
in the world. Even the premier intelligence

agency on the planet, the Israeli Mossad, got their equipment from the same source.

He started by hunting for bugs using his Micro Bug Detectors (audio/video), room by room and determined to scan every inch of the house. He had always been a man possessed with protecting his family.

After thirty minutes of searching in every nook and cranny, dislodging spider webs and moving even heavy items out of place and searching underneath, he sat down at the kitchen table with two items that looked like insect twins—two audio detectors. One had been found in his office, the other in the master bedroom.

He grabbed another bottle of beer from the refrigerator and waited—it was close to one o'clock. The devices could have been from another time, previous occupants, or it could be a gift from some pervert getting their kicks. Chad did not want to think it was someone at the base checking up on him…although he had done the same thing to the homes of others. That's why he couldn't dismiss the possibility happenstance.

At one forty-five, the phones burst into their annoying chirps. He was sure it was not an emergency call from the base, confident Carla would have covered for him.

Nonchalantly, he picked up the corded receiver from the wall phone. He only used cordless phones when corded were unavailable and said, "Buford—"

"Hi, Hon., I just called your office and Carla said you had gone to the house…are you all right, are you sick?" She was nibbling at her lower lip, a habit when feeling apprehensive.

"Sure…I'm fine, just had to get out of that place and clear my head…you know, get away from all the politics attaching themselves to the military." He considered telling her about the bugs, but then he wasn't done and it really wasn't a good conversation considering she was probably on her cell.

Sarah's voice relaxed as she continued, "I got a call from Marissa Manning. She asked me to meet her for lunch, of all places at the O-Club on base." She paused, "Did you know she's a captain?" She waited…even though she knew there were things Chad could not tell her, she still got irritated when she felt she were being deceived or just not included.

"Actually, I just checked her file at work, she's a reservist, just like us, only she's with the Air Force…probably a political appointment of some kind, Sarah…but I'd rather not talk about those things over the phone…okay?" There was a lot more he wanted to say, but circumstances would have to be different. He hated being clandestine but it was for her safety—and his. Chances are the bugs were recent plants, but why?

Chad could almost see her lips tighten as she said, "Oookay, we'll talk about it later." She didn't know what was going on, but this furtive behavior was one of the reasons she had left the intelligence business. Only, sometimes, did it help her to remember how frustrated her mother used to get when her "undercover cop" father would keep secrets from her mom. Sarah's mother had come from an affluent, but not gaudy-wealthy, Philadelphian family. Her mother just couldn't resist a young Marine named Hornsby, so in the end her mother had become Amelia Beckworth Hornsby, family black ewe. "Do you have to go back to the base right now?"

"Maybe for another half hour or so, that's all." He glanced at the noisy battery-operated wall clock, "See you in twenty…okay?

"I'm on my way."

Chad put down his bottle of beer and began rescanning the house. He had known surveillance workers who put timers on their devices. When one set of the bugs was detected, it triggered a timer that waited and then activated another set of devices. By putting in a delay switch, a person would think, after a scan, the house was bug-free and get careless, assuming that was it. Chad was not going to let that happen to his family. It took him less than fifteen minutes to determine everything seemed clear. Normally, he would ask himself *why* there were listening devices in his home, but he was not overly surprised…what mattered at this stage was *who* placed them in his house and how current the activity. It could be the military or a rival agency, even a foreign spy, but what seemed interesting was when the two bugs looked more like hardware that an amateur civilian would use.

Sarah had a few *secrets* of her own, not exactly secrets but questions that were bothering her. Marissa had invited her to lunch, but the time together was not just girl talk—some of the time seemed like a disguised interrogation. Some questions were about her time in the military, what she did…how she liked it and so on.

Marissa even asked Sarah about time in high school and college. Specifically, Marissa wanted to know what she knew about Heather DeVunder. High School was a time Sarah never liked to discuss, even with Chad. It had been a sad time when the Hornsby family moved to Pittsburg—her father had just died from a gunshot wound and they had gone to live with her Grandmother Hornsby who lived in Pittsburg. Whenever the subject of college came up, she just repeated what the files at OU had said about her and her subjects.

The door swung open and Sarah looked around the room, "Well, I see you found the refrigerator…how's the beer?' She laughed with a girl-giggle she knew Chad loved to hear. "Got one for me? Sure could use it."

Sarah let out a sigh of resignation indicating bottled-up exasperation. "Marissa talked my ear off…make that *ears*.

I'm glad for what little you told me about her, but, hey, she's nothing like I expected."

He pulled a set of bottles from the fridge and said, "I'm sure this won't be a short conversation…I'll get a couple of glasses." Chad shook his head and grinned, "What'd you expect?"

"Oh, you know…the usual. How're the kids? Who're you sleeping with; sort of a combination of Opra and Dr. Phil— That kind of thing."

With an amber bottle poised in his mouth, Chad nodded then put down the bottle. "Okay, so what *did* she talk about?"

"It was more like an interview…an interrogation. She asked lots of questions about us, the kids, my background and it made me feel uncomfortable, the way she was doing it, I mean—" She propped her feet up on the footstool and examined her toenails as she wiggled them. "I need a pedicure."

He snickered at her consistency—she always had this way of switching subjects in mid thought, it used to irritate him, but now he just found it adorably female.

"I've got a great idea to get your mind off all your confusion."

She narrowed her eyes and tilted her head, then one eyebrow went up. "Why, major, are you trying to get fresh with me?"

"No, Ma'am…I was not trying, I was merely suggesting; how about a team shower, sort of a recon in force?" He moved closer and gently placed his hand under her chin. Softly he kissed her puckered lips and placed a hand on the inside of her outstretched thigh.

She checked her watch, soon time to pick up the kids from school. "I'm afraid you'll have to wait at least fifteen…seconds, Sir." Sarah put down her drink and made a seductive run for the stairs leading upstairs and to their bedroom. She giggled, "Catch me, if you can!"

More than once, Chad had won a bet he could disrobe in less than six seconds, beating her time by a full second and no matter how much of a head start she managed to get.Taking the steps two at a time, he grabbed the handrail and pulled up as he took the distance in stride, dashing headlong to catch his playful wife who, by this time, was past the upstairs hallway bathroom by a step.

Two glasses of slightly consumed beer bubbled away: alone and unfinished.

Down the street, a dark green pickup truck pulled to the curb and parked. The two people inside studied the Buford residence. The key question was, "Had she told anyone else?"

Chapter 7

Sarah Buford was running a few minutes late. The kids never seemed to mind as, routinely, they just played with the other children while waiting for the arrival of their tardy parents. She was reflecting on her time in the shower with Chad, as she treasured such playful times. It just seemed that, lately, their lives had gotten so serious, so all of a sudden. Maybe it was because of the kids or the job…but she felt the fun times were becoming less and less.

The first thing she noticed upon arrival was the school bench seats were empty. *Strange indeed,* she thought, and so she pulled up in front and stopped her car. *Where are the kids?* Sarah looked all around but could not see Warren or Glenda. She got out of the car and looked over the tops of the shrubs, still no children. By the swings she could see one of the teachers walking toward her. *Are the kids hurt?* She wondered. *No, the teacher's not running.*

The teacher began talking from a distance away, "Mrs. Buford…Warren and Glenda left with Carl and Betsey Manning…I hope it was all right." Reading the disapproval on Sarah's face, she said, "Oh, dear, I hope I haven't done something wrong."

Quickly, the teacher spoke her reasoning out loud and provided some vindication, "The children asked if they could, and they said you wouldn't mind. She was going to take them straight home." The teacher held up a hand as if she were warding off a blow then said, "Mrs. Manning suggested it…she said you two were friends… Oh, dear! Have I done something wrong?"

Without answering, Sarah got into her car and slapped it into drive. She was as furious as she had ever been in years, <u>furious </u>at the children for going with a stranger, <u>furious</u> for doing something without permission, and angry as hell at the gall of Marissa Manning to assume the kids' parents would approve of such a thing. Her mind was full of dark thoughts— had the children been kidnapped? Did she take them with the idea of using them against their parents? Was Marissa trying to show Chad what an irresponsible mother Sarah was by pulling such a stunt? The fact was, Chad was partly responsible for her being late…so was that the plan all along? Her insides churned with confusion, hate, and thoughts of vengeance, but most of all she wanted Warren and Glenda safe and at home.

Sarah's car raced down the highway at a high rate of speed when, abruptly, she decided to make a left turn just two blocks from their home: she almost overshot the intersection. Quickly, she jammed on the brake in an effort to negotiate the tight left turn. Behind her, a dark green, six-passenger pickup truck responded to Sarah's abrupt deceleration, the truck tailgating too closely behind.

Sarah heard the screeching of tires and instinctively looked into the rearview mirror, further impeding her turn due to the delay in reaction time. Her mouth dropped and her eyes widened as she realized she was going to be hit. Behind her, the tip of the hood and the windshield of the coming vehicle were all she could see…heading straight for the back of her car.

Several blocks away, on the front steps of the Buford home, Marissa Manning and Peterrr Buford were chatting when they heard the crash, a hard thud followed by the raining of glass and screaming of tires. Quickly, a plume of smoke began rising from the direction of the sound.

With his hand covering his eyes from the Florida sun, Chad whistled in mock gesture, "Sounds like a bad one… I hope no one was hurt."

Marissa glanced behind her and checked on the kids—all four were present. "Curling smoke is never a good sign, Major." She gave him a polite smile and motioned to her children, Carl and Betsey. "Okay, guys, let's go."

Without looking back at Chad she mumbled, "Sorry I missed Sarah … I had a great time this afternoon, she was a lot of fun."

After her children were loaded in the car, she moved her mouth close to Chad's ear, "I can see why Heather liked you, too bad she was hung up on your brother." She then turned about, got in and closed the car door… With a wave at Chad, she pulled away, leaving the column of billowing smoke in the other direction.

It had been a long time since he had heard the name, Heather DeVunder… Chad was not sure why Marissa DeVunder Manning had said what she did, but it didn't sound good. He waved an off-hand goodbye as the car disappeared around the corner.

Warren and Glenda went inside the house to hunt down some milk and cookies. The earlier crash sounds emanating from the direction of the smoke gave Chad Buford a bad feeling in the pit of his stomach. He didn't want to believe it was Sarah, but as the seconds passed he got more concerned.

When he couldn't take it any longer, he grabbed his cell and tapped up his memory bank, the number for the school illuminating in front of a blue background. He selected the number and began to pace about his front lawn as his eyes glued to the direction of the smoke, the faint odor of burning rubber and oil still heavy in the air.

When the school answered, he could hear a background of children laughing and shouting. "This is Mister Buford, Warren and Glenda's father… Is my wife, Sarah, still there?" He held his breath as he waited, praying she was still on the school grounds.

"I'm sorry, Mister Buford, but she left about ten minutes ago…she seemed in quite a hurry."

The angry, ferocious animal in Chad's stomach took a big bite—fear was eating him alive. He didn't like Sarah talking on the cell when driving but sometimes it was necessary. Each time the phone rang and she didn't answer, he could feel the noose of panic tightening around his windpipe. Part of him wanted to dash to the scene of the accident and another part of him was terrified at what he might find, always a possibility though maybe, just maybe, she needed his help. Unable to take the pain any longer, he decided to get the neighbors to watch the kids while he went to investigate.

Not wanting to worry Warren and Glenda, he made the excuse that he needed to go to town to talk to one of the officers from the base, and he would be back soon.

Slowly, he drove down the road, every turn of the tires bringing him closer to discovering the truth, which is what he feared most.

The area was covered with emergency vehicles, curious people making nuisances of themselves, the police and, of course, the bloodthirsty media. The thick, black smoke painted the site in a light coating resembling smudged ink, and the flames, dissipating some, resembled those of a campus pre-game bonfire. Between the flames and smoke he could see their car, now barely recognizable. The six-passenger pickup truck had not only hit their car, it had shot into the air and now rested nose down, on its back side, leaning against a telephone pole near street side. The speed at which the pickup was traveling rendered it a flying missile and it had penetrated halfway into the trunk of their family auto. Chad braced himself for the worst as he stopped his car, got out after forgetting to shut off the engine but managing to put it in park and setting the emergency brake and ran hard to the accident. *What the hell happened?*

"Hey, Buddy, get back—" an elderly policeman shouted, his arms waving.

Chad shifted his path toward the officer, "Officer…that car is mine, my wife was driving it." He paused, "Did she make it?"

The words stuck in his mouth, his eyes beginning to smart from the stinging fumes.

The old man softened as he shook his head, "Sorry…I don't know, Mister. Check with the EMTS. Over there!" he said, trying to be as polite as possible.

Chad began to make his way in the direction of two ambulances parked on the opposite side of the billowing smoke. The officer lifted a strip of yellow barrier tape labeled in large, black letters. The word was POLICE, but it might just as well have said DEATH.

Picking his way through the myriad of standing gawkers mindlessly moving about as if they were watching the latest reality-based TV show, it was difficult for Chad to move around the cameras and endless news people. They had positioned themselves between the accident and emergency crews trying to save lives and control the raging fire. The inferno was now spreading toward the nearby homes and landscaped properties and a few roofs were smoldering.

A bright light moved into Chad's face and a voice challenged him, "Excuse me, Sir, what do you know about the accident?" The smiling news lady appeared as if by magic, she pushed her hair behind one ear and moved closer to Chad. She tilted her head to assume her best camera pose, "Aren't you Major Buford from Eglin base? Is this accident scene a matter of security, Major?"

He would have liked to punch her in the mouth, but that would have to wait, as he knew getting the press on his side could be critical if the accident turned out to be serious. "I know you want to help, but my wife might have been in that car… Please excuse me; I'm very worried about her."

Chad dashed toward the ambulances, his heart pounding from bad thoughts thrashing through his mind, but he was not aware of one single beat. Only the picture of Sarah's sweet smile kept him going.

Mesmerized by the burning vehicles, the crowd stood shoulder to shoulder as they watched the fiery carnage gain again in ferocity. Looking like two prehistoric creatures locked in a clutch of death, the smoke and fire cracked and hissed as flesh and blood of plastic, oils, and cloth dissolved into a new threat, sending rolling waves of gray-black smoke into the late afternoon sky.

With a sharp slamming of back doors, the two ambulances quickly pulled into the nearest traffic lanes, perched on top of the trucks, the emergency lights came on and began to spin and blare, demanding everyone notice the importance of their mission—to get the crash victims—or victim—to the hospital as quickly as possible.

It was a feeble attempt, but Chad made a short dash to catch up with the departing ambulances. Even if he had caught up with them, it was doubtful they would have stopped to answer his questions or even permit him near the patient or patients. Chad pulled up and bent over to catch his breath, as he looked over his right shoulder when he felt the touch of a hand.

The voice was compassionate, "Hey, Chad, are you all right?" Peterrr Manning bent down to place his head alongside Chad's. "What's going on…you were after that ambulance as if it were life or death."

Chad took a deep breath, turning his face toward the pavement under his feet. "I've got to find out what happened to Sarah…she could be in that ambulance." He straightened up, "I've got to get to the hospital… but which one?"

Manning turned to one side and nodded toward the burning cars, "Is that your car?" Incredulity seemed to highlight his every word. "Was Sarah driving that car?"

"Jesus, Peterrr, give me a break… I've got to get out of here and no one seems to know a damned thing. I've got to find out about Sarah."

Grabbing Chad by the arm, Peterrr said, "My car's right here… Get in! Besides, you're in no condition to drive."

Peterrr began driving in the direction the ambulances had taken and together they turned to the shortest route to White Cliffs Memorial Hospital, the trauma center for the local region.

"Hell of a crash, Chad, but I'll bet you she's all right… I just know it, probably just a hell of a case of whiplash."

Chad appreciated Peterrr's attempt to cheer him up, but right now he just wasn't in the mood to be cheered up. "…I hope so."

Chapter 8

With the children next door and no one home, the figure entered the back door and quickly made way down the hallway and crossed to Chad's office. Moving to the side of the desk, the figure crouched down and a small device was plugged into the back of Chad's computer…intended to transmit online data without the knowledge of its owner. When finished with the mission, abruptly, the lithe silhouette dashed across the room and out the back door and made way across the back yard into the nearby woods. Transmitted data would have to be analyzed, collated and perhaps decoded before it could be sold or used, but the thought of financial reward far exceeded the possibility of being caught.

Known for its role in developing and testing of nonnuclear Air Force armament, next generation precision-guided weapons and even intelligence (C4I) aerospace navigation, drones and guidance systems, such software was a veritable candy shop for spies and criminals. All past projects paled in significance when compared to the cornucopia which could be found with *Project Black Hole* and its spin-offs…at least that is what she had been told.

The home of Major Buford was just one of many places where information was simultaneously being gathered, but without gaining such information, legally or otherwise, they would open themselves up to greater costs, time delays, and most certainly the possibility of exposure and sure loss in a burgeoning market.

Warren Buford stepped out from the closet in his father's office as he watched the figure disappear into the woods behind the house. At one point he almost came out to challenge the known person, but his instincts stopped him. He was not too sure what he should confess to his father when his father returned…maybe nothing. His father didn't like it when Warren played in his office, much less when he messed around in his office closet. As long as the figure didn't know he was in the office, he wouldn't tell on the person and the person wouldn't tell on him. Maybe he would ask Hillary Blain at another time…

From the back door of the house, Warren turned around and walked to the desk. Even for a youngster, he knew quite a bit about computers, but he could not see what Hillary might have done…possibly nothing. After looking around, Warren decided that whatever she had done, it must not have been very important. *Maybe all she did was get some part numbers.*

Without giving it another thought, he went to the backyard and began seeing how high he could go on the family swing set. He was supposed to be at the neighbor's house, but they only had a girl…that was okay for Glenda but boring for him. *What's keeping Dad and Mom? They should be home by now,* Warren muttered to himself as he went higher and higher on the swing.

Chapter 6

The emergency room at the hospital wasn't as bad as a front-line combat hospital—but it was close. Chad Buford was surprised at how many patients were being shifted about by people who resembled shoppers at the local supermarket, not indifferent staff but a veneer of cold professionalism tempering outward compassion. Everything was habitual, nothing seeming routine.

For the second time today, Chad was rebuked. "Sir, please wait at the reception area…this space is for staff and patients only." The five-foot one-inch female orderly shot him a look that conjured the image of a six-ten male on loan from the WWF.

Chad wanted answers. He had no idea if Sarah was even in this hospital…nobody seemed to know anything useful. "I'm looking for my wife. She was involved in a car accident…I think she might have just arrived in one of your ambulances."

"I'm sure you are, Sir, but I have to ask you to leave this area. Please inquire at the admit desk…over there," she said, pointing a pudgy finger in the direction of two swinging doors resembling the entrance to a restaurant's meat locker. "Please, Sir…we have patients who need our help." For the first time, he detected a note of compassion and decided, this time, to listen.

Reluctantly, he turned and walked toward the doors, but not before raising on his tiptoes to look around…no Sarah. *Maybe she wasn't hurt. Maybe she's at home now. No, that can't be as discharge would take a lot longer than this…* For the tenth time he tried her cell phone, then tried home and got the recorded message.

It was difficult to get anywhere near the reception desk. Whole families were jammed together, just like the crowds at the crash site. They acted like a mob of panicked animals fleeing a forest fire, and he was one of them. Behind, he watched as two ambulance drivers began making their way through the horde.

"Did you bring in a woman who was injured in a car crash?" Chad noticed his voice was shaking and he sounded short of breath.

"Yeah, Fifth and Wagner…lots of smoke."

"I'm looking for my wife."

Do you know the name?"

Chad gulped, "Sarah Buford?"

The two men looked at each other—it was not always a good idea to tell people anything about those whom they transported. Sometimes the person could be a lawyer, an angry husband after his wife, a nut case faking a relationship for some surreptitious reason.

He could read their faces: they wanted to say something, but it was one of those things that was a hospital no-no. "Look…" Chad pulled his wallet from his pants pocket, "here's my ID… Did you bring my wife in?" He further pleaded, "How is she?"

"We'd like to answer you, Mister, but it could mean our jobs. We can say…perhaps it's possible. We brought in a man, a pedestrian, and a woman, all involved in a rear end collision at Fifth and Wagner… But you need to check in with admit." Without another word the two men disappeared behind the doors.

Spotting an opening, Chad pushed his way to the counter, "I'm here to take care of my wife's medical bill and admittance." Chad was certain they would search their records for someone who wanted to pay a bill and was instantly amazed at the attention he received. "Buford…Sarah Buford."

Licking her ink-stained fingers, the receptionist began shuffling through what seemed like an endless pile of multicolored forms. Finally, she paused, "Sarah Buford?"

"Yes, she's my wife."

"Nope, no Sarah Buford—" She made a feeble effort to stack her pile of papers.

"She would have just come in. She was in a car crash."

The lady bristled, "Why didn't you say so?" She could not have been more curt if she were a civil servant. Pushing back her secretary style chair, she got up and went to a sliding glass window and began digging in a stack of documents waiting to be entered into the computers: many of them had smudges of bloody finger prints. "Ah, yes!" she announced triumphantly as she waddled back to her chair. "How do you plan to pay for this?"

Chad was astonished at her first question. Not, "How's your wife, or how are you doing…" Rather just a simple, "Show me the money" attitude. He knew not all receptionists were like this, but this one was. "I'm covered under the base's medical." He pulled out his medical ID. "Can you tell me where she is? How is she doing? Was she seriously injured?" He fired the questions so fast he was not sure she understood his plight. Chad felt a nudge at his left elbow.

"She's over here, Chad. She's been asking for you."

Unable to believe his eyes, Chad Buford stood examining the face of Peterrr Manning. *Why the hell was he still here?* "Where is she?"

Peterrr turned and began a swift pace toward a series of stalls separated by shower curtains like panels of heavy duty plastic. "I was on the way home but heard some more about the crash on my police scanner. They mentioned Sarah was here…I just decided to help you find her."

Chad felt stupid. He had a scanner, so why didn't he think to use it? Then he remembered—it was in the car with Sarah. "Is she all right?" his voice shaking, but he didn't care. "I've been worried sick. I was afraid this was the wrong hospital." He could feel his eyes begin to mist and droplets start to trickle down his cheeks.

"The Docs haven't said…they're still checking her out." Peterrr pulled back the curtain as he said, "They're pretty sure the baby is all right—"

It was impossible for Chad to comprehend the words Peterrr just spoke— What *baby? …Sarah hadn't said anything about a baby.* He wanted to gasp but that would be the wrong thing to do in front of Peterrr. She had   matted blood in her hair, and what looked like windshield cuts on her face and arms…he could not see the extent of her injuries. Now was not the time for panic or emotion.

"Hey, Hon, how're you doing?" He could guess what the real answer was but, right now, there was a need for comfort and re-assurance. Tubes and monitors were beeping and dripping, doing their job of keeping her comfortable—and possibly alive.

Sarah parted her lips, but nothing came out. It looked like she was trying to mouth, "I'm sorry." She tried to move her arm to reach out to Chad, but she only managed to move her fingers.

Softly, gently, Chad touched her fingers and held her cold trembling hand in his warm, healthy hand. He wanted to cry, but settled for giving her a tender kiss on the forehead. "It's all right, Hon…You're going to be okay." He moved back so she could see his face and he managed a reassuring smile. "You're just a little banged up." He winked and watched as she tried to smile, but the facial movements were too painful. He knew what was going though her thoughts and he answered to himself somewhat, *When the swelling goes down, you'll look just as pretty as ever.* Chad shook his head and grinned, "I don't know how you do it, but, right now…well, you look kind of sexy, Babe."

She moaned as she, again, tried to stifle a smile. She mouthed, "Liar." She looked like she was going to say something else, but a green-coated lady physician moved between them. "Mister Buford, I'll have to ask you to let her rest now. She needs to rest."

The physician checked a few numbers and made some notes on a chart. "May I speak with you a moment?"

Chad shrugged and blew Sarah a kiss and said, "I'll be back later, Hon…get your rest." He started out of the cubical, but turned his head to say, "The kids are fine. I'll explain everything to them. You're doing fine." As he left her bedside, he felt physically ill…he should be with her,-- she needed him.

Some distance from Sarah's earshot, the doctor stopped and turned to Chad. Peterrr was still trailing behind her. "She's in no immediate danger, Mister Buford, but the next twenty-four hours are critical. Right now, saving the baby is secondary…do you agree?"

Regardless of how Sarah might feel, he said, "Absolutely. Her life is what's important." He paused, "Does she know she's pregnant…I didn't…at least she didn't give me any clues.

"Women usually have their reasons, Mister Buford. Maybe she was afraid to get your hopes up." She placed her hand on his wrist, "Some women feel it's bad luck to say anything before the first trimester is over…she's probably just a little short of two months." She flashed a cheering smile, "Anyway, I'm sure she will give you her reasoning in due time." Abruptly, the physician turned and walked away.

Peterrr Manning had been standing back and off to one side, "Guess the doc got a call." He put out his hand, "Well, congratulations, Major." Peterrr tried to sound as cheery as he could under the circumstances. "Let's get you home."

Chapter 10

Glenda Buford was watching her brother, Warren. He seemed rather preoccupied…could it be because of the announcement their mother was going to add another baby to the family? It was supposed to be a secret, but it was three days ago their mother had gone into the hospital because of a car accident. That episode had now been overshadowed by the excitement of the coming event and Glenda looked forward to having a little sister to play with her. "What are you brooding about, Gloomy Gus?"

"Nothing!" he said, the words dripping out his mouth. The phrase was like some rehearsed line from a stage play. The truth was…he had not told his father about Hillary's visit and what she might have done…that was three days ago and now it was even more difficult to tell his father, as each day his sin seemed to get larger. Some might call it guilt, but that was only part of it, as he felt he was betraying his father. Warren wasn't supposed to ever play in his dad's closet. His dad had lots of "special" stuff in there. Now there was this baby thing. He wondered if the baby would replace the misbehaving child he had become.

The chiming of their front door bell interrupted Warren's journey into self-castigation. "I'll get it!" He jumped to his feet and dashed to the door.

"Hi, there—" An affected Marissa Manning tipped her head downward in order to examine the almost twelve-year-old before her. He knew what she was thinking; *He was short for his age.* "I brought Carl and Betsy over to play with you two…is you sister here?"

Carl and Betsy burst past their mother and into the house. While Carl grabbed Warren, Glenda came rushing to the door to meet Betsy.

From the kitchen, Chad came out and into the archway of the living room, "Hey…what's up." He glanced at the sets of children dashing off to various parts of the house. His eyes avoided Marissa as he studied his hands being dried by a white and blue checkered dishtowel.

"Just came over to give you a hand with some of the housework…I know how you men can rise to the occasion, but I'm sure Sarah would appreciate a woman's touch on the housework while she's recuperating." She hesitated and glanced around the room,

"My… it looks quite tidy. Anyway, the kids will be out of your hair for a little while."

For a few seconds, Chad felt a bit awkward—it would be difficult to refuse her help without engendering a few questions. "Ah, well, yeah, sure…glad to get some help. Right now I'm finishing up the dishes from last night's spaghetti fest." He still avoided looking at Marissa, but it was hard to do—she was outfitted in a yellow halter top which barely held in her breasts, and her short-shorts displayed most of her long, well tanned tennis legs.

"Got anything to drink…I could sure use a vodka martini." Marissa moved into the room and glanced toward the false bookcase. "Sarah told me about your wine cabinet."

Without a word, Chad removed the book cover, exposing the glass door.

"Wow, that's a nice stash of wine you've got! …Any Chardonnay?" Her head bobbed up and down as she looked over the choices. "Oh, here's one."

The one she picked was an expensive French import—his face flushed as he moved toward the cabinet. "That's a pricy bottle, Marissa."

"Oops, sorry… Maybe a martini would be a better choice." She turned and walked in the direction of his office…it was where the liquor cabinet resided. "Your place is laid out just like ours." Marissa glanced back over her shoulder and did a Marilyn Morrow pose, "Actually, I'm more of a martini girl than expensive grape juice." She laughed and started examining the counter top, "Great…and the ice?"

Chad was beginning to feel uncomfortable—he looked through the French doors and watched the children playing on the gym set in the backyard. "Where's Peterrr…is he on base, I need to thank him. He really helped me the other day."

She snorted and started fixing her drink, "Want one?" Her eyebrows moved up as she began shaking the mixer. "I never know where Peterrr is…he's his own man. We have that kind of marriage, you know. 'Don't ask, don't tell.'" To avoid any further conversation in that direction, she turned her attention to the kids playing outside, "I better go check on the kids. I don't know about your two, but mine need a few reminders and occasional reprimanding."

He was always cautious. Chad didn't believe in coincidents, at least not the awkward type. If Marissa chose to be here, at this house and this time, it was for a reason. Being a man, he could appreciate the questionable implications, but, if anything, his life did not need any more complications, much less an explosive affair. "I'll finish up my dishes…then, if you're going to be here for a little while, I need to run to the base and meet with a few officers." It would be a way to get some work done, and avoid encouraging Marissa.

"Don't let me run you off. I'm not going to embarrass you…Chad." She paused to observe his reaction. His face softened as she smiled and almost whispered, "Heather told me you were a shy-guy."

He smiled, "Yeah, your cousin was a sweet kid…that was too bad about her accident, but I hardly knew her." He bobbed his head as if remembering something. "Actually, this gives me a chance to catch up on some of my work…I haven't been able to get anything done since Sarah's crash." Chad avoided mentioning his talk with Sarah—

she had been hopping mad about Marissa
picking up the kids. "A couple hours…no
more…okay?"

"Yeah, sure, but you'll owe me?" She
licked the inside of her martini glass and
grinned. "Hurry back." She paused and
almost shouted, "Anything about the other
driver?"

"Not a clue…he seems to have just
disappeared. And the strangest thing of
all—the truck was stolen. The police are
working on it but figure it was one of those
'undocumented people.'" By now his skin
was beginning to crawl. He had heard what
a vixen she could be but wanted to believe
she had put that aside…for Peterrr's sake.

"I'm going to swing by the hospital and
check on Sarah." He turned and headed for
the door, "I hope she can come home later
today, or tomorrow at the latest."

Marissa did a slight slouch and pushed her
lips into an exaggerated pout, "Poor
hubby…lonely all ready?" Then her face
changed, almost theatrical, "You know…I
was with Heather when we both were
thrown from our horses. A mountain cat
frightened them, maybe a fox they think.
Heather hit her head on a rock, but it was

her horse's back hoof that crushed her skull. I was thrown, face first against a tree that had just been pruned. Those branch stubs cut up my face. I'm sure you noticed the scars."

He just shook his head, "Not really, Marissa…they did a good job." He knew she was not really apologizing for her appearance, rather fishing for a compliment or hidden reaction. Chad smiled and then silently moved through the door and hustled to his car. It felt good to get out of the house—and away from Marissa. She was a strange person, but he wrote some of it off to the accident. She was a woman, and they cared about their looks…Sarah had often reminded him.

Chapter 11

Eglin Air Force Base was hardly a household name— Seldom mentioned in the national news, it sported ten landing/takeoff fields that did everything from serving as Navy platforms known as Choctaw OLF, to highly classified Research and Development (R & D) of weapons, communications, tactics and the occasional unmentionable project. Under this scrutiny, however, anonymity would seem impossible. Perhaps it was good management, remote location or lack of interest by the press.

Chad headed due north of Field Four where the civil engineers and service mobility training guys do their thing, straight to Field Five, known as Site C-4, his final destination the microwave station.

For almost a month, he had received tips that information on Project Black Hole had been seeping into the intelligence community—possibly nothing more than a rumor, but probably the truth…the question would be, as it always was, *who* and *what* had been compromised.

Chad was not an engineer, nor was he a technician, but he was very successful at finding leaks and the bad guys causing the leaks. Whenever possible, he avoided "wet work"…he was a hunter, but he preferred to kill his game only when necessary, not murder it. He enjoyed a good hunt—when the game was played well, like an exhilarating game of chess. The stakes were higher in the world of cat and mouse in real life, however.

Chad's mind wondered back to one night when he and Sarah cuddled up on the couch and listened to some soft classical music. His mind reverted to autopilot as he maneuvered down the road and he thought about the sipping of wine and talking about the quirks of life...

"Sometimes it's like I'm dealing with rain...night rain."

"Night rain?" Sarah shifted her body and gave Chad a quizzing look. "Did you say, 'Night Rain?'?"

"Yeah." He laughed, "Like night rain...people." He took a deep sip of his Merlot as if tanking up for a long explanation. "Did you ever notice how it is when a light rain falls at night...while we're sleeping?"

"If you're really sleeping, Chad, you don't hear it." Sarah shook her head at the foolishness of his statement. In a soft voice she muttered,"Night rain people."

"Exactly, Sarah, you don't hear the night rain people, but in the morning you see the evidence of what the rain did during the night. That's how you know that the rain

was here, that it did something... The night rain people come and go as silently as a gentle night time shower. It's my job to find out where the rain fell and why—and if we hadn't been sleeping, we probably would already have the answers."

Snapping out of his reverie, he turned left on a hard-surface dirt road that would take him to a manned guard station—Chad figured he would never get much further than the cafeteria. He intended to meet with the security chief and discuss the rumors about information being leaked from the post under that security chief's scrutiny.

After checking in at the guard station, he made his way to the cafeteria and got a cup of coffee while he waited. He flipped open a folder labeled *Project Black Hole*—it wasn't the project's real name, but it gave everyone a point of reference.

According to the pieces of information Chad had picked up, whatever the project was…it could become the ultimate weapon—literally capable, with one strike, of destroying a pack of cigarettes or a complete planet—at the user's discretion. The weapon was somewhat expensive to make, but cheap to operate. He had heard them bandy about the code name Maelstrom—and Chad suspected it might be the real name, or the name of a piece of the project.

He could sense it…there was something going on at the base. Everyone he met was uptight about something—like just before some high ranking officer was coming to check things out—like the CNO.

"Sorry to keep you waiting, Chad…or should I call you Major Buford? How is Sarah?"

The voice came from behind Chad, but he knew the voice, "She's fine…thanks for asking. Since this is at a military base and about a military issue, I guess you can take your choice, but I'm being paid as a civilian advisor. He put out his hand and met the firm hand that was extended, "Good seeing you, Peterrr…or should I call you Captain Manning?" Chad looked around, "Where's your boss?"

"Occupied, Chad. Colonel Blain always has his nose in something." Peterrr Manning paused and leaned forward. "I think, by now, everyone knows about it." Peterrr took a long pause as he looked around the room, "but last night three of our technicians were kidnapped, or kid-something. This morning we found one of them dead at his home…apparently injected and interrogated."

Major Buford's eyes narrowed— "So the project's been compromised?" Knowing nothing about the missing techs, he just decided to play along. He was wondering how such a thing was possible. In the intelligence business they had a motto, "It shouldn't be a possibility."

"Well…we don't know that for certain."

"Your techs don't live off base, so how did this happen?" Chad scribbled a reminder to check about the housing arrangements. Sitting back in his chair, Peterrr sighed,

"Yeah, technically that is true, but when the techs feel the need for some 'companionship'…well, we can't bring any partners on the base so we bring them to a safe-house in town." He read the concern on Chad's face, "We vary the houses, and this is the first time something like this has happened."

Quickly, Chad interjected, "That you know of..." He took a gulp of coffee and resumed talking, "Why wasn't I told about this?"

Just as quickly, Peterrr retorted, "Why didn't you know? Aren't you the one who is supposed to find out about potentially vulnerable procedures?" It wasn't meant to be a snide dig, but then, there was no other way to say it."

There was a slight nodding of Chad's head as he said, "Okay, I see your point. I need to look into that…later." He tossed his pencil onto his notebook and studied Peterrr Manning. "All right, let's move on…what about the other two missing guys?"

Peterrr winced, "They were abducted from the base…about ten-thirty hours last night. Nobody heard a thing."

"Abducted from the base, not town? No clues?"

"A set of tracks show two people probably each carrying a person," Peterrr shook his head and went on, "but here is where we got lucky."

"Lucky?"

"Yeah, those sleeping quarters are usually occupied by…let's call them Bob and Bill. Bill is a top notch Doctor, one of our best. Bob is more of an assistant and new to the project." He paused and murmured, "Bill was working on a test and didn't want to interrupt his research. He decided to work late. Here's where we were lucky—Tom, another assistant, was taking a break on Bill's bunk." He chuckled then said, "They took two assistants and missed Bill…probably the real prize they had targeted. Oh…and all three of those names don't necessarily mean they were all men."

"So, where did the tracks go?"

"Toward what we call 'the cave'…it used to look something like a busted gold mine… I think they were extracted from the base by a Blackhawk helicopter, or at least a stealth plane of some type."

Peterrr watched Chad's reaction…was Chad buying the story? Chad saw that Peterrr's facial expression was devoid of what one would expect to be "more bravado."

Chapter 12

In the middle 1800s, the little "gold mine" was at the far end of nowhere, not intended as a real mine at all—more than likely used by pirates as a place to hide from the British,

French, and other opiates of society. Later, it was a place for smugglers to stage shipments of liquor being smuggled in from Cuba, Europe, or Canada. Chad pulled up to an area surrounded by tropical brush and short Palm trees.

Major Chad Buford had considered telling Peterrr, Marissa was at his home taking care of the kids but had a feeling Peterrr already knew as much. However, did Marissa know that Peterrr was at Field Five, C-4? She claimed she never knew where he was—they were a strange pair.

Two guards snapped to attention after Chad presented his identification. The ground was peppered with markers made of various colored flags and it only took a few minutes for him to question Peterrr's statement the people abducted could be women, unless they were very large and heavy women. Inside the cave the ground was moist—the smell mindful of a rancid chunk of canvass. At one corner, next to the entrance, was a pattern of three imprints which formed a wide triangle—probably from the feet of a camera or telescope tripod or a harnass pickup…now marked with a metal pole holding a colored triangle. The peculiar thing was there were no footprints where a person, using the device, would have stood—odd, but he speculated it had to be explainable.

Back outside the cave, Chad took note of the footprints left by the guards and then the exterior of the cave—after years of disuse, now supported by makeshift wooden supports and bits of canvass (which explained the smell). He now was having a problem understanding why this spot had not been bulldozed over—after all, this was a highly secured and secret site.

Moving away from where the guards had been, Chad popped out his cell and called home—Glenda answered, the other children were squealing like they do when they are dashing through a shower from the garden hose. "Hello…Buford residence, Glenda Buford speaking."

Sarah had taught the children to use polite telephone manners when answering the phone, but Chad preferred the children not give out so much information before they identified the caller. "Hi, Pumpkin, it's Daddy. Is everything all right?"

She giggled; her high-pitched voice reflecting a jubilant mood. "Of course it's you, Dad… We have caller ID." She turned her head and yelled at Warren, "Warren's being a brat, Dad. He's not playing with Carl, and he's just pestering Betsey and me."

Chad thought Carl Manning might be a bit introverted. He muttered to himself, "That's my boy." Raising his voice he said, "Get Mrs. Manning on the phone…will you, Sweet Pea?"

"Sure, Dad." The phone clunked as she set it down on the end table.

Immediately the voice of Warren Buford shouted into his ear, "Hi, Dad. Carl's playing with a frog he found in the back yard…and the girls can't hate me chasing them…they're laughing, Dad."

"I know, Son. I've played that game before…you chase them and they pretend to not like it…you'll get used to it."

"Here's Mrs. Manning… Bye, Dad." In the background he could hear the shouts of two harassed girls and the battle cries of the two boys.

Marissa sounded as if she had been working over the liquor cabinet, or was it just that he expected to hear her slur words. "Got stuck at the base, huh?" She sat down and leaned back in the overstuffed chair. "The kids have been fine…Carl is trying to get his frog to race like the story by Mark Twain. Warren is terrorizing the girls…and I'm cleaning out your liquor cabinet while straightening up the kitchen."

Rolling his eyes and picturing the scene in his mind, Chad let out a strained laugh. "Yeah, well you know how it is. I came out to check on something and walked into a hornet's nest." Like any experienced interrogator, he started laying the groundwork for his main question. "Have you heard from Peterrr?"

"Not a word… for all I know he's in the Middle East or Corpus Christi of all places. Hell, he could even be at the base, Chad." She paused, "So what's your interest in locating Peterrr?" Chad hesitated so she asked, "Why don't you just call him… I'm sure you guys have ways to get a hold of one another. You know…telephones or secret decoder rings."

Chad wasn't sure what he had learned— was *she lying, and she knew where Peterrr was, or just testing me?* He thought. "Yeah, I was going to do that, but I just thought while I had you on the line, maybe you knew where he was?" *Well, that didn't go as well as I would have liked.* "I'm leaving the base and going to the hospital to check on Sarah…will you be okay with the kids?"

"No problem… Tell her I said, 'hi.'"

He was still holding the phone to his ear when the line switched to a hum. After making some notes and taking a few photos with his cell, Chad walked around the mound and saw the spot where they believed a helicopter had touched down. The problem he was having involved trying to figure out how any aircraft could get in and out of the area without being picked up on base radar—there were few areas on earth as well protected as was this base. Maybe it *was* recognized and just written off as one that strayed out of its approved flight path.

There were a million possibilities, but Chad was beginning to believe the two missing technicians were probably already dead. It was even quite possible no one would ever know the truth about this incident—for all he knew, they had given out information and our government had stashed them some place or dumped their bodies into deep water or the everglades.

A soft humming sound was coming toward Chad and he turned to see what it was—moving fast and close to the ground… It resembled the noise of a large toy airplane or model car or drone. Chad froze…he could not decide what to do when seeing it approach. It was a drone airplane scooting over the ground—about ten feet high and sixty yards away. At a local park he would not have been concerned, but this drone could be armed, and out of control or a worse scenario—it was coming straight towards him on purpose.

He jumped to his left just in time to avoid a hail of projectiles spitting from the underbelly of the sand-colored craft. The unmanned aerial vehicle (UAV) banked right and Chad ran for the entrance to the cave—not that it would hide him from the infrared search or heat seeking equipment probably on the UAV but at least it would give him a chance. He was barely inside when he heard the pellets striking the sand and wood around him—one even grazed his ankle.

The soft noise of the drone then began to fade—it had either landed, gone higher to wait for him, just left or remote control was rendered useless due to the cloaking features of the cave walls. *What exactly had just happened?* Chad asked himself. He knew they tested UAVs at the base, but this area should not be one of the places. The big question was—was it intentional or accidental. The drone could have honed in on Chad's cell. Was he expected to be written off as a "training accident"? *Where the hell are the two guards that were stationed by the cave?*

Peeking out of the entrance to the cave, Chad could see a HumV making its way toward the cave. *This is either good or bad— are they coming to see if I'm dead?* He decided to wait until they got closer before he would come out of his protective hole. His nostrils itched and felt clogged with dry mucus from the stale insides of the cave.

Two men jumped out of the combat vehicle and spoke before locating his position in the cave, "Major? Are you all right?" The young corporal was dressed in desert fatigues—on his arm was the band of an Air Patrolman…AP, the MPs of the Air Force. The driver of the vehicle was trailing behind the other policeman.

"That drone is a hunter-killer, Sir…experimental, supposed to be five miles to the east of here. Are you all right?" The corporal looked over Chad as if examining him for ticks.

Right now, Chad wasn't sure what he should say. He was shaken, but couldn't admit that. He was furious, but understood the problems of experimental projects. If it had been a serious attempt on his life, it was a clumsy one…and most likely was only meant as a warning—but why? "Corporal, I would like to see a full report and copy of the tracking log for that drone." Chad paused to dust off his coat sleeve, "Not because it almost killed me, but to get a picture of the damage it has done to a crime scene." It was a lousy excuse, but, under the circumstances, the best he could do. "Give me a lift to the O—Club." He needed a stiff drink.

After a few soothing drinks, Chad settled down and was considering the events of the day—the chance visit to the microwave site, and then contacting Peterr Manning. Then there was the news about the three technicians—one dead…and the other two, unnamed sexes, were missing…or dead. Of course, there was the errant drone…that just happened to go off course and decided to use him for practice—accident, coincidence, warning, or a blundered attempt to wound him? He was leaning toward "a warning" and he set down his drink and began rotating the glass about—he was glad the drone was not running in silent mode, but now wondered if Sarah's car wreck had really been an accident. Of course, it could be he was just paranoid about it all…but in his line of work, paranoid was good…it kept people alive and caught bad guys.

Chapter 13

He wasn't sure he should be driving—his hands still seemed a bit shaky and he had been sipping drinks for almost an hour. He should have made a report to the AP's Officer-of-the-Day (OD) but wasn't ready to give a rational report of the incident, thus showing his cards to who knows what. After the drone incident, there was little doubt in his mind but what he needed to find out more about Sarah's "accident"— especially since they had not located the driver of the stolen pickup truck. The common explanation was, because it was in Florida, some illegal person was driving the truck and didn't want to be found out—plausible, but too convenient to satisfy him in light of other unexplained incidents. There was also the conflicting report there was a man *and* a woman in the truck. For now, he chose to believe his "accident" had occurred when the drone had been drawn off of its target because it picked up a false read from Chad's cell signal.

With only a little effort, Chad found a parking place in a far corner of the hospital parking lot. He shut off the engine and leaned back and took a deep breath, as he didn't want Sarah to see him in this condition—hands shaking and decidedly edgy. He closed his eyes, but the image of the drone bearing down on him was riveted in his brain…it wouldn't go away. The whole thing was like a computer stuck in a loop—he could swear he could still smell the gas discharged from the drone's cannon. He willed himself to get out of the car and make his way to the elevator—there was no way he could recall driving to the hospital…so riveted was his concentration on the drone, like a mental blackout.

The doors opened and he stood like a cigar store statue, as if in a trance…he wanted to move, but he could not make his body respond to his conflicted state of mind. It was then he realized something…the bullets were not meant to *hit* him—they must have released some sort of chemical or electronic signal intended to interfere with his ability to think or move.

When the doors began to close, two white-suited men stepped into the elevator and one of them pressed a button—the panel above the door registered a B and the elevator was going to the basement. He was blacking out.

Like a helpless puppet, he allowed the two men to move him to one corner and roll up his sleeve…he didn't feel the needle professionally inserted into a bulging vein at his elbow. The men were talking, but his senses were either scrambling the words or they were communicating in a foreign language unfamiliar to him. Chad was feeling better—his mind was beginning to clear, but his body still felt weak—he opened his eyes.

Major? Major? Major, how are you feeling?" the sandy haired man in the white jacket said, slapping Chad's forearm… It was beginning to hurt.

The other man was outfitted with thick glasses that looked like they had been stolen from a 1950s rock star. "I think he's coming around…look at his eyes."

A short stream of liquid squirted from a syringe held by the sandy-haired man, "Another shot?"

"I don't think so." The black-rimmed glasses man moved closer to Chad and flashed a penlight into his eyes. "Yes…he is definitely coming around."

The doors to the elevator glided opened and the two men grabbed Chad under the arm pits. The basement was more like a parking garage—cars and trucks lined up neatly between little yellow outlined rectangles. The air smelled of wet concrete mingled with oil and gas fumes, but the floor had been treated with some kind of epoxy which made it resemble the glass top of a coffee table or supermarket.

Chad could see the men were taking him toward a vehicle outfitted like a state-of-the-art hospital van. It was a putrid green color resembling guacamole barf. The thought made Chad smile…he was feeling better and could now move his fingers and feet. His whole body felt like his mouth did after getting a shot from his dentist, but his body was starting to come back the same way his lips would. He tried to talk, but nothing would come out, yet.

"Don't worry; Major…you'll be okay soon." The glasses man was looking into his eyes and doing the penlight thing again. "You are in no danger, and we have someone making sure your wife is safe."

He was being stretched out on a gurney and belted so he couldn't move. He managed to mumble, "Safe?" The effort was incredible, but the result was encouraging.

"Yes, safe…we'll explain as soon as you are out of danger and coherent." The redhead provided a friendly smile and patted Chad Buford on the shoulder. "It'll be okay…you'll see. You're safe and we're the good guys—"

Carefully, the two men slowly draped a thin white sheet over him. "Right now you should sleep…we'll talk when you wake up."

Major Chad Buford felt himself drifting into unconsciousness. He wondered if he were dying, but then he knew he was worrying about the kids and the vamp that had overrun his home and inserted herself into his life. They said that Sarah was *safe*... Now, what did that mean?

The last thing he saw was the memory of the sand-colored drone tracking him down as if he were a hunter's evening dinner. After one small shudder he was greated by a bevy of soft clounds to a place called 'dreamland'.

Chapter 14

Sarah suffered from a severe case of restlessness from lying immobile in a hospital bed—she was a doer, not a procrastinator. A few minutes before she had received a call from the base and was told Chad had been unavoidably detained—he would call as soon as he could. She looked over at the young Marine who was dressed in starched fatigues—apparently her husband felt she needed a babysitter. "Sergeant, could you bring that phone a little closer, the nurse moved it when she brought in my breakfast."

He gave her a polite smile, "Certainly, Ma'am." There was no doubt but what the sergeant was good at his job—otherwise he would not have had his rank at so young an age.

Sarah was a reserve officer, and the wife of an officer, but her greatest pride was as a good mother…right now, she missed her children—Warren and Glenda, her prizes, reward and the second greatest reason for getting up each day. Chad had chosen her…the children were hers by the process of birth. She punched up the number for her home and a woman answered.

"Hello? Major Buford's home… Mrs. Manning speaking." The voice sounded casual even a bit too laid back.

Sarah flinched— what *is THAT woman doing in MY home? Was that why Chad had not been to see her?* She controlled her voice, "Marissa…what a surprise. On the phone you sound a lot like your cousin." She wondered why she said that then paused and said, "I would like to speak to my husband." The selection of the phrase *my husband* was deliberate…a reminder to the invading female that Chad Buford was already taken.

Marissa sighed, "So would I. I got here over three hours ago…I thought Warren and Glenda could use some company. Carl and Betsey are here." She paused and spoke to someone…it was Warren, "Your mother is looking for your father…you can talk to her in a few minutes."

Eagerly, Sarah asked, "How are the kids? Are they playing nicely with Carl and Betsey?"

"Yeah, but *your husband* disappeared to the base right after I got here."

Good for Chad! "You don't say…he does that to me all the time." Sarah smiled, noticing that Marissa didn't ask how she was doing. That in itself was a bit strange.

Another sigh, "Yeah, Peterrr is always doing that to me too… You'd think I'd get used to it, but you know these…men." After saying the word, *men* she made a sound like someone who had just had her mouth stuffed by a bar of soap or a barnyard product.

Not really interested in Marissa's home life and Sarah made no comment. "Have you heard anything from Chad?"

"Well, I'm confused, Sarah. First Chad called here and said he was going to visit you at the hospital…then I get a call from the base saying he has been tied up in one of those damned meetings." She broke with an audible deep breath and a sigh, "Hell, I don't know what to do… I've got to do some shopping at the base commissary."

Sarah was about to giggle—if she read Marissa right, she was not to be trusted…she could be wrong, but not likely. "I have a young lady I use when I need to get away…I'll call her. You might know her, Colonel Blain's daughter, Hillary?"

"Warren mentioned Uncle Blainy's daughter…is that she?"
"Yeah, that's Colonel Blain, all right, obviously he's not their real uncle, but the kids really love him." Sarah paused, "And, Marissa…thanks for caring about the kids, I'm sure they are enjoying the visit."

"Hey, anytime I can help…let me know." She paused…the line had an awkward moment. "Ah, want Warren now?"

Fat chance in hell I'll let you know if I need help! she thought. "Yes, please, put him on… and thanks again." She wanted to talk to Warren and Glenda, but she also was concerned about Chad—the situation wasn't unusual, but it was just one of those gut feelings.

Finally, Warren got to the phone. "Hi, Honey, are you having fun?" Warren began to rattle off a bunch of things that only meant he was enjoying himself by pestering the girls. Then she spent ten minutes listening to all of the outfits Betsey and Glenda had tried out…they especially loved trying on Sarah's shoes—of course they had put all of them back.

Like a phantom, an elderly nurse came into the room and checked Sarah's chart and, except for a nod to Sarah, who was still on the phone, it was as if the room were unoccupied. She checked on the drip solutions and then drew a syringe from her pocket and pressed its contents into Sarah's IV line.

"Mommy's tired now, Glenda…I'll call back later." Sarah was feeling deliciously relaxed…every muscle in her body felt as if it were on vacation. Her fingers fumbled as she tried to put the phone back in its cradle—the nurse, with the sergeant standing by, took the phone and gently placed it where it belonged.

A picture very quickly took shape—a pond…and two figures hitting a man as he slipped below the pond of ice, the scene followed by a murky pickup truck.

The ceiling was stark white, bright enough to offend Chad's eyes. He blinked and narrowed his eyes as tightly as he could. "Where am I?" he said, his voice firm and clear.

In one easy movement he sat up and began to look around his polar ice sheet, white surroundings. He was in a standard sized hospital bed in a gigantic room—in all he counted thirty beds. Only one other bed seemed occupied, at the other end of the room—a pale blue curtain which looked like *shower curtains* used by hospitals: the only thing obstructing his view. The thought crossed his mind—was this a horror movie film set and he was part of the team of actors, playing out some grotesque dismembering scene.

"Anybody here?" Chad asked in a polite hospital voice. No answer. At the foot of each bunk was a footlocker…against the wall, a metal wall locker…he was beginning to believe he was at some military hospital, perhaps in the Iraq war zone. When he placed his bare feet on the concrete floor he was surprised at how cold it was—the touch sent a chilling jolt up his legs.

He pulled open the metal door on the wall locker behind his bed and heard the familiar vibrating sound made by locker doors. His clothes were on hangers and hung in military fashion with the left sleeve facing the open door. Quickly, he slipped into his clothes—the first thing he wanted to do was test the doors. All of the walls were pictureless, whitewashed concrete. The metal door was cold and would not yield.

"Locked and no windows," Chad muttered. He thought about pounding on the doors, but felt better about it when he noticed surveillance monitors tracking him—they knew he was there and he was up and about. His leather soled shoes resonated as he padded his way about the rectangular room—he would check out the other patient…maybe that other person would know something. Chad was filled with unanswered questions and he didn't like it…*I wonder how Sarah and the kids are doing?*

Sideways he slipped through the opening in the pale blue curtain. The beeping of the monitoring equipment was like a metronome orchestrating the vital signs of life. With just one glance he realized-- lying in front of him was his precious wife, Sarah. He froze as if he had just seen a magnificent painting. He wanted to grab her, to hold her, to shout out his feelings of relief, but he would have to wait until she awakened. She had not put on make-up or any of her usual one hour morning treatments, but she looked beautiful to him—he fought back the impulse of unmanly tears.

She would have been furious to know her mouth was hanging open, just a bit, and a soft snore…more like a purr, was singing from her parted lips. He kissed her forehead before he settled into an overstuffed chair obviously placed there for just such a purpose. No doubt, the safety of Warren and Glenda would be something she would want to know. He would say the kids were safe…at least that is what he would tell her; their duet of Warren and Glenda had told him.

He settled back in the chair and began to speculate. What in the hell was that stuff, or thing, they used on him? What was going on? Sarah moaned in her sleep, the way she often did when they were at home…he felt his pulse rise as he hoped she was waking up—it seemed there was so much to talk to her about. She turned onto her side and continued her rhythmic breathing. He made a mental note to talk to Lieutenant Colonel Blain…affectionately known to the children as Uncle Blainy as he was also the father of their babysitter, Hillary Blain. Maybe Uncle Blainy could shed some light on these bizarre events.

The life of Chad Buford, Sarah, and their children had just taken some sort of turn—he had not yet figured out what had happened, but he had a feeling it was related to some of the new weapons research going on at Site C-4 on Field Five. There was no proof to back up his hunch, but it was possible, more than possible. At this point he wondered if Peterrr and Marissa Manning had anything to do with what was beginning to look like a shadow military operation. Whose side they were on was another question. Sarah turned her head toward him and blinked her eyes.

Chad jumped to his feet and rushed to her bedside. Delicately he reached for her hand—it looked so small, white. An IV tube just below her elbow made him flinch inside—he felt guilty that she could be in pain and there was nothing he could do to take the hurt away. "Yeah…it's me. How're you doing?" He smiled and mustered his most reassuring smile. "You look great."

Her voice was raspy and weak…even a bit ethereal, but beautiful to Chad, "Oh, WOW, where am I?" She barely moved her head as her eyes slowly wandered about the room— her gaze rested on Chad, "Back in boot camp?" As if seeing Chad for the first time, she closed and reopened her eyes slowly, "Chad?"

"Yes, Sarah?"

"Are we at the base hospital?" Sarah glanced around.

He had no idea, but not wanting to alarm her, he patted her hand and spoke very softly—he was sure they were being monitored. "Yes, Dear… You're at the base hospital, but just for a checkup."

"I want to go home, Chad. How are the children?" It was as if she hadn't heard a word he had spoken.

"They're fine…they miss you too but want you to rest and get well. That was quite a hit you took, but you're going to be okay. You just need lots of rest." Now that she seemed more lucid, he wanted to ask her what she remembered about the crash, but he resisted his inclination to act as an investigator. At the moment, she needed a husband…not a probing policeman. "Right now you need to rest." He repeated his words and watched as she closed her eyes and settled against her firm pillow…deep asleep.

There was no sense in trying to find a way out of the block-walled ward. When they wanted him out of the room, they would get him. Chad returned to settling back in the overstuffed chair. In his gut, he was not feeling as much fear as he was curiosity—if "they" had meant to harm him or Sarah they had already had ample opportunity. No, this was something else…they wanted something, or wanted him to do something—at least he hoped it was as simple as that.

In time, there was a click like the sound of a muted loudspeaker. A soft, feminine voice said, "We would like to speak with you Major…would now be a good time?" The solicitous voice paused.

Chad wanted to test what devices were in place so he nodded and said nothing.

"Good…please go to the double doors just past your wife's cubical."

That meant they had video surveillance. He got up from the comfortable chair and took another look at Sarah. He wasn't sure what was going to happen, but he was going to do everything he could to insure her safety. He believed, once he stepped past those double doors, all of the events of the last three days would make sense—he only hoped it would be for the better.

Chapter 15

Peterrr Manning had spent the whole day trying to track down Chad Buford. The drone incident at the base cave had been written off as a transmitter error on a piece of test equipment, but it had almost killed a reserve officer and was not to be just

sloughed off. The additional problem of
Major Buford being a high-profile expert
with an enormous amount of field
experience raised other issues—if there were
something untoward, Peterrr would find it
out. For the fourth time he called the Buford
home.

"Buford's…with whom am I speaking?"
The voice was crisp and officious.

"Captain Manning, Miss. Is the Major in?"
Peterrr was not sure who the lady was, but
the voice sounded like the same girl with
whom he had a previous similar
introduction. He was certain she was in her
early twenties, maybe younger.

"No, Sir, he is visiting with Mrs. Buford,
Sir. I believe they may be on their way to
Boca Raton or Miami for a medical
consultation."

Now he was sure the voice was either a
military or a young low ranking secretary.
"Is <u>Mrs.</u> Manning there?"

"No, Sir, she said she was going shopping,
Sir. My father is Lieutenant Colonel Blain,
Sir, and I often babysit the Buford children.
I am Hillary Blain, Sir." She paused to
await a response—there was none. "I would

be glad to take a message if you wish, Captain.”

The emphases on rank was one of those things bratty military kids often did…it was meant to put the lower ranked person in their place. The intent didn’t escape his injured ego.

“Oh, yes, Hillary…I believe my wife has mentioned you.” Peterrr hesitated and then answered her offer to take a message—it was a mixture. “No, but thank you, Miss Blain…but I guess you could tell the Bufords that I need to get in touch with the Major.”

“Will do, Sir.” She hung up the phone and snickered, if only to herself. She turned around and clapped her hands—Warren and Glenda smiled. “Well, now Hillery bent down and grinned…who would like some… macaroni and cheese?” Hillary didn’t really know Marissa, but she hated her anyway. She had heard Marissa had a reputation for making passes at men, even her father. Maybe the tales were true, maybe they weren’t. She didn’t care. Lately, Marissa had been spending a lot of time with Lt. Colonel Blain. It was true Hillary wasn’t sure where the Bufords were, but she didn’t mind—Warren and Glenda were fun to babysit.

"Can I cook the *Mac,* Hillary?" Glenda had hopes of being just like Hillary when she grew up. Without waiting for confirmation, Glenda changed subjects, "Will Uncle Blainy be here?"

"Not today…mind the hot water." Hillary looked around, but could not find any writing materials. "I need a pen…I'm going to your father's office. You two be good." As she left the room she glanced over her shoulder to see what kind of cooperation was going on. *That's it…teamwork, works every time.*

The Cheery Room is what Hillary liked to call it, the office dutifully appointed with group pictures of the family and special events of Warren and Glenda. Hillary dropped into the high back leather chair and pulled at the center drawer—it was stuck. At first she thought it was locked, but when the side drawers opened, she knew the center was jammed for sure. Her real name should have been Curious Hillary…at least that's what her mother used to say. She dropped to her knees and moved behind the center drawer…something was stuck against the top edge of the wood. She checked the computer…the device she had so carefully placed was still there. With her thin fingers she reached up and pulled down a little box…not much larger than a quarter and a little thicker.

"What 'cha doing under there, Hil?" Glenda was crouched at her feet.

Hillary Blain began scooting out from under the desk. "It looks like…I think this must have slipped out of the back of your Dad's desk." She gave it a curious look, "He might have been looking for it." She also knew her father, LT COL Blain, told her to keep her eyes open for bugs and traps…*"One never knows when someone is trying to steal information, Hillary. Keep a sharp eye,"* *he had said.* She pretended to return the device to its place at the back of the drawer then opened the drawer as if nothing had happened. After taking out a pad and pen, she left one note—the one about Peterrr's call. She patted her pocket to make sure the device was okay.

Warren came dashing into the room, "Hil, you got to see the neat job we did…lots of butter and extra cheese."

"I grated some cheddar to go on the top," Glenda said, making sure she got credit for her extra effort.

"How about a couple of HOT DOGS?" Hillary knew the answer but loved to hear the kids squeal.

"Yaaa!" Warren, Glenda and Hillary exchanged high fives.

Hillary could only wonder about the little black object at the back of the drawer…it deffinately was not something she had put there.

Chapter 16

Like a set of heavenly *pearly gates* illustrated in an old time movie, the double doors opened to allow Major Buford to leave the dormitory room. A short corridor could be seen; the concrete floor painted a light blue and slightly sloped upward. He moved slowly, cautiously, taking in all the surroundings—there was not much to see, but that told him something too…the place was like a prison…perhaps a fortress of sorts?

Ahead, a door opened and he turned right and passed a group of five men who stood like figurines awaiting the arrival of a playmate. Chad was surprised by the comical effect—their faces were covered with Halloween-like masks that depicted various famous look-a-likes.

"Where's mine?" Chad tried a little comic relief. "Got one of Humphrey Bogart? I always liked him."

The five figures rewarded Chad with polite laughter and sat down while indicating the chair in which Chad should sit. Judging from their uncovered arms, one of the five was a woman…possibly married, with a black faced Omega watch which he considered could be a deliberate clue, offered to throw him off.

The first man to speak sounded like one of the men who brought him to this place. "We want to apologize to you for the theatrical way, in which we brought you here, but we were concerned for the safety of Mrs. Buford and yourself…and, may I say, we are concerned for our own safety as well." The speaker paused as if expecting a response from Chad, but Chad just sat in silence. "We want to assure you that you are in no danger here and your wife is receiving the best of care. It appears she is recovering nicely and all that remains is for her leg to heal. At your wife's request, Hillary Blain is taking care of the children. We have also posted a few people about your neighborhood to…shall we say, 'take care of things.'" Again the voice paused, "May we now get down to business, Major?"

All his life he had been trained for just this kind of situation—now Chad's brain was recording information as fast as it could. The room, the people, even the type of pens and pencils that were being used. "Okay…if I believe we are in no danger, why am I here? Why were you concerned for our safety?" He did believe them, and he had plenty of questions to ask to pry open a corner. Chad had only a hunch why he was there, but he could wait.

"We need your help, Major." This time the voice came from the end of the table, Chad did not recognize the person behind the mask. "It was our intent to ask you for your help, but it was going to be a little later. Last week's events made it imperative we change our time table, although we would like to believe some of it was serendipitous."

"Last week's events?" Chad said, tilting his head and waited for clarification.

Another voice began speaking from behind a Catherine Hepburn face. "I'll try to give you the abbreviated version, Major." It was the woman with the Omega watch—her voice was clinical and distinctly influenced by some other language…maybe Slavic. "The drone that chased you uses a magnetic bullet. It disrupts the electrical flow of the human body…depending on the magons from the Nano-structured magnets. Originally, we were researching the technique for medical use…it was intended to reduce or eliminate pain during surgery. Medical procedures could be performed without the use of current drugs."

Science was not his field of expertise. He understood why magnets worked and the fact that the human body is a chemical-electrical mechanism, but "Nano-structured magnets" and 'magons' were another thing. "Keep it simple, Doc."

"We short circuit the body's nervous system…it causes paralysis without killing the subject." She paused and wiggled her fingers—obviously a nervous gesture. "Depending on how strong we induce the… magnetic field's intensity, ampere per meter, it can range from a short blackout to death."

Chad shrugged, "So…what's the problem? Why am I here? It sounds like a good weapon, and probably cheap to produce."

Again the voice at the end of the table spoke, this time the sound was slow and rather edgy. "Yes, yes, you're right…Mr. Buford."

This was the first time he had been addressed without his rank of major—and the gesture probably meant something. "Thank you…I thought I was confused, now I *know* I was." He chuckled—more to relieve his nervousness than to enjoy his statement. "So, what's the problem?" Chad searched the inscrutable masks for any clue to the persons behind them. Nothing;no one responded.

Suddenly, there was a feeling of tension in the air—the silence was vociferous. The voice continued, "What we just told you was for your information…call it a trust gesture, Mr. Buford." The speaker paused—making sure everyone was listening. "How do you feel about a weapon which could quite possibly destroy our planet with the touch of a button?"

"You mean like a hydrogen or neutron bomb on a gigantic scale?" Chad had to grin…how long had he heard that story and how long had he thought it possible to achieve? "Okay…such a thing is possible, but we all know it comes under the category of *unlikely.*" *If this is the problem, this is going to be a waste of time,* Chad told himself—*a dull journey into ifs and supposes.*

The man leaned forward and placed his forearms on the table—they were thin and decorated with brown colored liver spots. "I understand your credulity on the subject, but how would you feel about a device that could be greater than…one hundred million times more powerful than the atomic bomb first detonated at Bikini Atoll in 1949?" He muttered something under his breath, "Huuh?"

Catherine Hepburn began to speak, "Major Buford, we are not talking theoretically as we have reason to believe such a device is being prepared as we speak. As a matter of fact, you have already seen the results of some minor events possibly triggered by a fledgling electromagnetic pulse beam, a Susame beam." Her tone turned to one of disgust, "What started out as a way to harness the many benefits of the sun has been hijacked to produce a destructive weapon. Are you with me now?" The question seemed to end with the unspoken words "There…I said it."

Heads nodded all around the table and there were low-level muttering and murmurings. For a few seconds it seemed as if everyone was talking at the same time, but there was nothing clear for Chad to hold on to. "Susa… you mean tsunami?"

"*Su-<u>same</u>* Beam, Major, not tsunami, as in tidal wave." The man removed his mask. He was one of the men at the hospital. "You probably could recall my face, so there is little reason to hide it from you." He stood up and walked to a pull-down map of the world.

It reminded Chad of when he was in high school and the teachers would pull down various maps or charts. "Am I going to get a history lesson?"Chad was still stuggeling with the very thought of such a weapon.

The abductor smiled and snorted, "Perhaps…but what I am about to show you is more than classified." He stopped and got very serious. "So far, all you have seen or heard is there are a bunch of mad scientists who are worried. We told you about a new magnetic weapon and the combination name of a couple of mythical Sun Gods." He directed his laser pointer at Chad and put a small red dot on Chad's chest. "What I am about to show you will create a 'no turning back point,' Major…do you want me to proceed?" He turned off the laser pointer, "We can stop here and take you back home…just forget about the whole thing. No one would believe you anyway."

This was not the first time he had heard this kind of a threat…as a matter of fact, in his profession, it was an all too common event.

"If this project is as important, and as dangerous, as you say…then, of course, I want to know about it. But only if you want my help and think I can really do something about what you call 'the threat.' If this is a clear-and–present' danger moment, then…"

"We believe you can be of great assistance, Major. We also believe you have demonstrated, if given the help you need…you can help us kill or at least delay the undesirable parts of this project."

"Will it be necessary to, as you say, 'kill' the project—perhaps it can be redirected?" Chad furrowed his brow and hoped the answer would be yes.

Catherine Hepburn interjected, "Actually, Major, we had considered such an option, but the potential for misuse is just too great…too tempting for the dregs of world society." She paused to take a deep breath—it sounded more like a sigh of disappointment than a need for oxygen. "I'm sure you understand."

"Okay…let's hear it." Chad turned his attention back to the world map, vowing he would reserve natural skepticism until he heard the whole pitch.

Chapter 17

All eyes focused on the wall as the world map was changed. "It was one of those serendipitous things, Major. The SOHO satellite was sent into orbit quite inauspiciously, but they had made certain adjustments in some components. At the time, you'll recall a cover story the press released to that effect. However, you did not hear about a rogue group that realized the possibilities of using the solar information in a different way. The intent was not to just gather information, but to investigate the possibilities of using the sun's unique properties as a controlled source of global energy and climate control. Some people want a station in space, while still others want stations on earth."

"Sounds good so far…so what's the problem?" Chad said, making his usual face of confusion.

"For chrissakes! Listen, Major, if it had been that simple, we would not be concerned. The SOHO is a satellite that observes and gathers information about our sun. Please pay attention to this map…it shows the known platelets of this planet." The man gave an intent look at Chad Buford…like a school teacher making sure that he was receiving the proper attention. "Now…as you know, the world's platelets, when they move too quickly, can cause earthquakes, tidal waves and, of course, tsunamis."

Chad registered a dutiful nod to indicate he was paying attention.

"The principle is simple, Major. Now, listen— I will try to keep it simple, possibly too simplistic, but bear with me."

"Lay it on me, Doc. I need to know your concerns and what you want me to do."

The man smiled, "Good…suppose we start with the basics. The core of the sun is like a fusion reactor that produces new particles, which is why our sun doesn't 'burn itself out.' These fusion stations emit gas…call it gas plasma. As the sun rotates faster at its center it interrupts the ongoing magnetic field…producing solar flares that send, we'll call them 'rays,' toward the earth. Our earth's magnetic field protects us from getting a full dose of such rays." The man lowered his voice, "Think, Major…what would be the effect if we got a full dose. Too much, we fry, too little we freeze…ice age all over again, and in minutes."

"Of course I can only guess, Professor. I'd rather you tell me." Chad had seen a lot of science fiction movies about death rays and magical beams that could destroy planets, but here, right in front of him, were a group of scientists telling him it was really possible. "Is this some kind of a Buck Rogers or Star Wars scenario?" There was no answer. "Are you telling me there are people…now, who are trying to interfere with our natural forces?"

"Questionable reports say that there have already been tests with this thing they call *Susame*. It's a combination name about an *angry* oriental sun god, Susano-o or Susa, and his *peaceful* sister, Amaterasu, or Ama. Hence, they get the name, Susame, but the real culprit is Susa. I'm getting off track, Major." He used his hand laser to point to the map, "We believe this device could already be responsible for a number of earth slide, volcanic eruptions, and 'unpredicted' tsunamis. Maybe even the scare of global warming." He lowered his pointer and shrugged, "Of course we have no proof…it is just as possible they are naturally occurring events. But when taken as a collective whole—"

Chad jumped to his feet, "You're telling me that our government is doing this…killing innocent people around the globe?" His face was red with anger, but he wasn't sure where he should direct his anger.

"Absolutely *not,* major…that is one of the reasons you are here. It is being done by a business consortium that claims 'to want' to develop the device and use it to give free energy to the world and stabilize our climate. However, now, it is in the hands of some who could want to blow up this planet if the rest of us don't succumb to holocaust blackmail on the scale of Biblical final events. Maybe only control things for their personal profit." He waited for the words to sink in. "The UN has told us they think our worries are unfounded." The lecturer hesitated, his voice lowered. "Have you ever heard of a person who goes by the pseudonym *Barnacle?"*

"No…never heard of him, but he sounds nautical. How did you come by the name?"

"The answer is twofold—one is…was a defector, now dead. You stumbled on the abduction site and soon after the drone went after you. It honed in on your cell phone. Another thing…we acted on the informant's intelligence and were able to intercept some transmissions that told us what they were doing." He pointed to Ms. Hepburn, "Would you please."

She stood and put her hands behind her back—she began to pace in a small area. "This consortium has run into some technical problems and needs some new parts in order to make more tests, so this has bought us some precious time. The obvious question is, 'Why don't we just shoot down their counterfeit SOHO satellite?'" She stopped and held up two fingers, "First…when it fires, it leaves no visible trail like a microwave signal…ah, or like watching an alcohol fire when it changes from yellow to white, then disappears. The intent is to disrupt the magnetic field of the sun and thereby produce a gigantic solar flair. It is our belief they expect to control the flairs by controlling the earth's magnetic field. If that could be done, then deserts could be productive fields of food or timber…it also means whoever controls the devices could turn productive fields into deserts…"

She paused for a drink of water. "To our way of thinking, *that* is a weapon. We don't know which satellite is the right one…there might be more than one. For all we know…everything might be being controlled right here on earth. So shooting down something in orbit might only serve to really inflame them, and the only way to guarantee 'getting it' is to shoot down all the satellites, thus nailing the buggers for good. But we can't do that, for reasons obviously political."

After displaying a shrug that showed her frustration, she said, "We have reason to believe that several of the latest catastrophes that appear to be temper tantrums by Mother Nature are actually the work of their Susame capability. Maybe it only nudged a natural event while they were experimenting. Either way, we don't know that." She placed her palms on the top of the table and looked at Chad. He could see her eyes narrow behind the slits in the mask. "Of course we can't prove it…and we can't officially stop them…there are international problems to be considered, repercussions."

Back to the unmasked man at the map, "That's where you come in, Major." He turned off his laser and put it into his breast pocket. "We want you to find out *how far* they are along and *how* to stop them before they are in a position to blackmail world governments or, worse yet, start global famine, from which there is no surviving. Just information…you are not required to do anything. We just need enough facts to confirm or refute our premise."

Chad moved his hand to the back of his neck and rubbed his hair line—it was a nervous habit he had when considering things. "I have several observations…first, don't you have it backwards? Aren't you supposed to gather facts and *then* arrive at a conclusion? Now, don't take me wrong, *but* how sure are you that they actually *have* one of these Susame Beams in place? Further, doesn't someone else already have agents in place to answer your questions? Sort of a government 'James Bond' already waiting and in the wings?" He rubbed his chin as he waited—and discovered he needed a shave.

"Yes, the United States Government has several agencies already investigating the Susame Project and trying to identify *Barnacle,* but as with most 'government projects' they fall far short of providing anything useful until too late. Look at U. S. Intel regarding WMD in Iraq the day before invasion— See what I mean? Do you get the point? Most of what we have received gives good indication that the CIA and FBI are quite useless when it comes to real end-time events. And this is what this is…real-time Armageddon.”

The Hepburn mask threw up her hands in frustration. Her voice became flat and very serious. “To tell you the truth…there might be a U. S. project under way, but no one wants to talk about that.” A hush settled on the room…everything seemed to be so quiet that only the noise of the air circulation system echoed in the room. “At first we thought it was a project by a foreign government…maybe China or a South American country, rich in oil and gold deposits. We hoped you might have some information concerning the project, but, apparently, you don’t or, you, too, are unwilling to share with us. Our conclusion is… it *is* probably a secret project in middle stages and run some by a rogue government or at least funded in the area of its black ops.”

“Maybe it’s just none of our business…like the ‘Manhattan Project.’ I mean, if we didn’t drop the big one on

Japan, the Marines would have had to kill its way in, inch by inch. So it doesn't mean that it is necessarily as evil as you think." Chad wasn't so sure of that, but he had seen lots of secret projects that not only failed but would never be used. "It's not the project that is inherently bad…it's the people and how they decide to use it. If it is for peaceful use and helps to solve a global dependence on fossil fuels or help the world's food supply…well, that might not be too bad." Chad waited for their response. "Of course it would totally destabilize the Middle East. Thinking on it a bit, Einstein left the Manhattan Project expressly because he saw the splitting of the atom was achieved solely for military purposes. To a great extent, he was right. Not that we don't have nuclear power plants…still the atom bomb was the end result."

"Fair enough, Major, but…what we haven't said is…while we may be working on the project…" The unknown face at the end of the table paused and looked around the room. "…we know, *for a fact*, the Chinese government is spending billions, maybe trillions of dollars to beat us in developing such a weapon or, perhaps, a

'peaceful system' using such technology."
He hit the table with his somewhat pudgy
hand and began to spit his words out in a
fierce rant, "Can you imagine, even
remotely contemplate, how dangerous this
would be to the free world, or how insane it
would be if two governments had such a
doomsday capability or controlled the
world's energy source? If nothing else…we
need to know if we will be able to preserve
our way of life—if and when." He pointed
his finger at Chad, "Do you realize what will
happen if this …thing…destabilizes the
magnetic belt that protects the earth? We
could go into an ice age or be fried like a
broiled steak."

The man at the map said, "We don't know
why, but someone…probably from the
Chinese government, Iran, or North Korea
thinks you know something about this
weapon. Your family is in grave danger,
Major—since they seem to think you know
something. Make no mistake about it—that
was no accident your wife survived. It is for
this reason we brought you and your wife to
this shelter…your children will be joining us
shortly, if you think it is necessary…and
why wouldn't it be." His voice shifted to a

soft mutter, "We need you on our team to help, if we are to find out what the truth is, and you need <u>our</u> help to keep your family safe."

What was he going to do? The whole thing sounded like some science fiction nightmare, but then, he was sure, the first guys that heard about the atomic bomb must have struggled with the weight of the information as well. Could these things possibly be true? Two governments racing toward a mechanism or even control of the world's power supply or caught up in the furver of 'religion'—that could not only destroy life, but enslave the entire planet…it was madness, absolute madness.

"I'm not sure I believe you completely, but it would be foolhardy on my part to not check into what you are saying. How do I continue to do my job at Eglin and check on this Susame thing?"

"That's easy," the unknown face said. "We think the project is being coordinated right here…under our noses. Do you really think that Site C-4 is only a microwave station? Camp Rudder has sent a lot of troops to Field Five for it to be just a field exercise… It looks more like a security team.”

Chad scowled and said, “Camp Rudder is where the U. S. Army 6th Rangers train. You’re saying they are sending men to guard the project?”

“Yes, I am, the unknown mask replied; I am not saying the men know what they are really here to protect. The mask paused, “One of us was killed trying to get the information we are telling you…two of us escaped. You just happened to stumble in on the ‘crime scene’ so to speak.” He paused to let his words sink in. “We hope we are wrong, but…well, in the normal duties you perform around here, you have access to things we could never see without arousing suspicion.” He folded his arms across his chest, “Will you help us, Major? We believe the head of the snake may be closer than we think.”

“On one condition—”He waved his hands high in the air and said, “If you will please take off those ridiculous masks… if I am as good as you seem to think I am, you must realize it would not take me long to track down each of you here. Do you really want me to waste my time doing that..just look at your hands." Chad chuckled to himself, *my god…none of you even bothered to put on gloves…your fingerprints are everywhere.* But they all heard what he said.

To a person, they all looked at their hands—there was a sudden silence which fell over the room. Of course there were other options open to the group—Chad and his family could just 'disappear'…or maybe they had sprayed their fingers with a plastic coating.

Chad broke the silence, "Look, it sounds like you have a legitimate concern, and I'll look into it. Just tell me where you think I should start."

All heads turned to the unknown face at the end of the table—the head nodded and everyone began taking off their masks. One by one they moved down the seated line.

One lone voice spoke out, "Find *Barnacle.* "

He did not know any one of them. Chad was surprised—not one face was like he thought it would be with most beyond the middle years. Only one figure did not unmask…he stood in the back corner, shielded by the shadows, and said nothing.

Chad looked at each one and said, "That's better...now let's talk— Barnacle.

Chapter 18

At first, Chad was concerned about coming up with a good cover story about the time when he and Sarah had disappeared, but, somehow; there were proper medical documents put in place explaining her emergency evacuation. They had thought of even that small detail. The papers said they suspected she had developed an aneurism and was rushed for emergency treatment. He chalked it up to the tendency of people to accept anything if the proper documents were in place.

* * *

When Chad returned from the family kitchen, he walked into their bedroom— happy to see Warren and Glenda up and about, sitting on the edge of Daddy and

Mommy's king size bed. In his hands he had a breakfast tray, some of Sarah's favorites. "What are you two rascals doing here—shouldn't you be getting ready for school?"

The kids giggled, "It's Saturday, Dad…we don't have school today!" chided Glenda. She jumped off the bed and rushed to inspect the food tray. "Pooh, burned toast…and the bacon is like a board, Dad."

"Just like your mother likes it, Little Lady." It felt good to see Sarah at home and the kids back to their smiling ways. "Now, don't be pestering your mother for food… Mom needs her nourishment so she can get back to being the family slave." He gave Sarah a quick kiss and set down the tray. She was not that bad off, her leg was messed up a bit and she had a few head bruises, but nothing serious. He had done his best to sell her on the story they had gone to a specialist to make sure she had no hidden head injuries—he wasn't sure she bought it but, at least, she didn't say anything…yet.

Preliminary research indicated the scientists were right—there *was* a project called Susame but foreign intelligence said it had been officially dropped from the government's 'miscellaneous' ops some time ago. What made him a little suspicious was there were no document files talking about the project; closed or open…everything was just a set of unsubstantiated rumors. In the past, this meant it was an experimental project which had looked promising but disbanded by the government and taken over by a government sub-contractor for further development. Chad had switched to the age-old adage, "follow the money." For the past few days he had begun carefully digging for a budget trail—there was always a budget trail…but so far, nothing.

"Well, Gloomy Gus, what are you thinking about?" Sarah took another bite out of her crunchy toast—it crackled like a pillar of ancient marble and crumbs fell on the tray. She had held her comments until the children had left the master bedroom.

He smiled and shook his head as if to clear it from the current subject, "Just work."

Sarah sipped hot tea and mimicked the way he shook his head. With her eyes fixed on Chad, she gulped down the beverage. "Something messed up, Dear?" Suddenly, she considered the children might be lurking about…she made a face and put her hand over her mouth. There was little doubt but what all the extra treatment was not necessary…she was totally mobile but knew Chad felt better giving her a little pampering…especially when he might need her to cut him some slack.

"Naaa, nothing special, just the same old routine—you know, checking documents on new arrivals, auditing inventories, monitoring transmissions…that sort of stuff. Rather boring, huh?" If things were as crucial as his panel of scientists seemed to think they were, he was going to need some help…but whom? Whom could he trust with this kind of project? He had considered Peterrr Manning, but he was not too sure about Peterrr's wife—she was nosey and too much of a social butterfly to keep things quiet. Another thing bothering him was-- she always seemed to be 'sucking up' to Colonel Blain. Still, in a way, it made sense because she had taken a course from the Colonel when he had taught a special class at her training center. Peterrr was good at his job, but still a question mark.

The day went by just like any other—he wondered why he had not bumped into any of his science friends…who now seemed to have vanished like yesterday's newspaper. At night he began having short dreams about a giant ray-gun zapping the earth and causing all kinds of death and destruction. If he were going to find out about this Susame thing, he would have to take a few risks—he had taken dangerous chances before but, for the first time, he was concerned for his family. It was clear from the accident the "bad guys" could get to anyone. Still, Chad had to admit he was having trouble believing such a project was credible, much less achievable. He had tried the library but it was no help…he would like to discuss the subject with someone else, but he didn't know whom he could trust. Tomorrow he would try something new, start covering the entire expanse of the base…field by field. He would stick his nose in and wait for someone to tell him that area was off limits, even to him.

Chad had tossed and turned all night…up and down to the bathroom and even late night TV in the living room with Closed Caption engaged. Sarah poured a splash of half and half into her morning tea and began stirring. "Okay, Chad, what's going on…?

You're not sleeping at night and now you're just staring off into space." She was glad the children were at school so they could speak more freely.

He ducked her question, "Look, Sarah, I will be a little out of touch today. I'm going to make a tour of the base, you know, just kind of catching up on what might need the attention of my crew."

She received his response as a deliberate evasion of the question. "Does this have anything to do with our stay at that weird hospital?" *To hell with being sensitive or discrete, I need to talk to my husband,* she told herself. "You just seem so…preoccupied." She closed her eyes and touched the cup to her lips, "If I didn't know better…I'd think there was another woman." She did the obligatory smirk and waited for a stern denial.

Chad rolled his eyes, "For God's sake, Sarah…gimme a break! You, of all people, know the nature of my work. I barely have time to sit and think much less fool around with some other woman!" He got up from the table and walked to the coffee maker, "You're a little edgy over the baby… You were the same with Glenda."

He was right, she had been a bit out of it, but this was different—Chad Buford was really bothered by something and she was going to find out what it was. "You're probably right, Dear…but I'm worried you're not getting enough sleep and we hardly talk anymore. So, when you're ready, how about talking it out with me?" She switched subjects, "When will it be time to update the kids about the baby?"

Chad shrugged… "We'll know, Sarah. My guess is the nosey little urchins already know everything." He planted a kiss on her soft lips, grabbed an apple and escaped out the door.

Alone in the kitchen, Sarah returned to her own problems. She could still see the face of the driver who hit her car…not the blur of another person or something confusing but the face of the man who tried to kill her. The face was older, but she thought she recognized it…If so, it was an easy guess why they had tracked her down.

Chapter 19

Field One was northeast of Eglin main—some maps called it Area C-5. To the observant onlooker, the entire base was shaped like a giant russet potato with a mouthful taken out of the middle. Chad was not surprised when he found nothing of interest…at least regarding the buildings at Field One. The area around the buildings was another matter, but he was going to restrict his first pass mainly to structures and keep an eye open for anyone keeping track of his whereabouts. Sometimes, the most revealing clues were things when they *weren't* where they should be—an unused parking lot next to a facility, a cafeteria that didn't allow off-scheduled backdoor deliveries, abnormal power consumption, just anything out of the ordinary.Such things could turn out to be more than just good clues.

In the afternoon, he scheduled himself for a run up Highway 285 to Field Two—ten miles north of the East Gate. During the mid 1970s, it was a Vietnamese Resettlement Camp. Besides located next to Field Three, the proving ground was inundated with the constant noise from the 919th Special Operations Wing and the 728th Tactical Control Squadron, all based at Field Three. At Field Two, it took him thirty minutes to get cleared by the East Gate guards, but that was a routine happening for infrequent visitors. It was well after 1700 (5pm) hours when he left Field Two, not that there was much to check out, but it seemed a good place to hide a research laboratory. The day had proved interesting, but rather boring.

Slipping onto Highway 285, Chad left the dust of dirt roads behind and headed home. He might not have found anything significant, but at least he had begun something—he was on the hunt, looking, thinking, sifting out possibilities.

When his cell rang he looked at the caller ID, "Hi, Sarah, just leaving Field Two…I'll be home in fifteen."

"Hi, Hon, just wanted to give you a heads up, Dear. Peterrr and Marissa are going to drop by and …let's see, how did she put it, oh, yes, 'Check in.'"

Chad had a slight edge in his voice as he replied, "Great…that's all we need, fix me a stiff one, Sarah, I'll need it." If there was anything Chad Buford did not need, it was Marissa Manning hanging around his wife—her very presence invoked painful memories.

"I'll make that…two for you and two for me." She shifted her tone, "Anyway, the kids will be happy…Carl and Betsy are coming too." She allowed her voice to fade off into a sing-song pitch.

"Well, at least it means they won't be staying long." He pulled out to pass a car creeping along in front of him.

"It's not a school night, Chad…it's a teacher in-service day tomorrow, so much for that theory." She finished with a mocking laugh. "See ya."

He watched as the slow car, now behind him, gradually disappeared from his rear view mirror. *Why were Marissa and Peterrr coming over? Just being friendly? Nosey? Intrusive?*

He pulled into his driveway and nudged up to the bumper of Sarah's replacement car. He had not told her, but her 'replacement' car, the one involved in an accident, had been outfitted with a GPS (Global Positioning System).

Ever paranoid, Chad believed the car which hit Sarah meant to do it, but when she tried to turn the corner too sharply, it hit her from the side back bumper. The reduced impact might have saved her life. The other driver had still not been found. The police were content to file it under accident involving an illegal alien, Chad was sure it didn't happen that way. He even considered it to be a hit with intent to kidnap or kill her.

"Hi, Daddy!" Two of the most lovely words he could ever hear, spoken by two wonderful children—not that he was prejudiced. "Betsy and Carl are coming over!" The kids were about to jump out of their skins.

Sarah handed him his scotch and water…no ice. "They're bringing Chinese…not the nation, just some food." She raised her eyebrows, "From our favorite takeout place…how about that?" She tossed her hair back in a playful gesture, "Pretty fancy, huh? Marissa said I needed a rest." She tapped her walking cast and rubbed her fertile belly.

The family was sensitive to Sarah's healing wounds—he gave her a gentle hug and a playful, sensual glance. "I certainly agree…for years, I've been trying to get you off your feet."

She nestled her chin into his neck, "Careful, Buster, you're dealing with a pregnant lady—we're famous for fierce behavior." She growled and purred.

Warren made a face and Glenda laughed and ran toward the window facing the driveway."They're coming"—a duet rang from the two greeters.

"Oh, goodie…better change!" Chad headed for their bedroom and flashed Sarah an impish grin and grabbed his second drink.

"Coward!" Sarah half laughed and soft-shouted out.

"Beware of 'Mans' (Mannings) bearing gifts, My Dear." Chad whispered as he closed the door to their bedroom.

The arrival of the Mannings was more like watching the Thanksgiving Day parade provided by Macy's. Warren and Carl came in followed by Sarah and Betsy, then Marissa, loaded with several cardboard boxes. Bringing up the rear was Peterrr who had his arms covered with paper bags decorated with fierce red dragons and filled with quart-sized white food boxes. The kids headed for the backyard.

Marissa set down her boxes and tenderly patted Sarah on her pregnant belly, "How're you doing?" She didn't wait for a real reply before she said, "A bunch of the girls put together some baby clothes and toys for your coming event… I know it's a bit early, but we're all excited and hope you'll be up for a shower…soon."

Sarah pressed a finger to her lips, "We haven't said much to the kids yet. If they hear the word 'shower,' they will bug me to death."

Marissa responded with a shrug and a scrunched, disapproving face. She whispered, "I think…even Betsey has figured it out."

"Step lively— Ladies…don't want the food to get cold." Peterrr looked over the top of the paper sacks, "Where's Chad?"

Sarah nodded at the doorway to their bedroom, "He's changing…he just got in the door."

"Yeah, you said he was at the base. I didn't see him all day…what was he up to?" Not expecting an answer, Peterrr inched his way into the kitchen.

"You'll have to ask him. He never tells me anything, Peterrr." She giggled and looked at Marissa, "They're so secretive." She knew Marissa and she were both familiar with the type of work their husbands did…everything was hush-hush and they bragged that their wives knew nothing. "Thanks for the boxes, Marissa…I'm sure I can use the stuff." *Probably not, but it was nice of them to think of it.*

It was ten minutes past eleven, or 23:10 hours, when the Mannings finally left. The kids had been starting to crump out shortly after ten. After that, long periods of silence were the norm…awkward because Chad was not willing to talk about his work, and Peterrr was being just as closed-mouth. Marissa and Sarah had a heated discussion about pregnant women and alcohol—they concluded it was nobody's business but the mother's and that *moderation* was the key. There was heaviness in the air, but it was doubtful either couple would have openly admitted it.

Susame, Susame, Susame! It was all Chad could think of, as his mind interplayed numerous conversations with itself. The scientists had spoken as if there were some urgency, but *how* urgent…and *where*, not a clue. He wanted to "follow the money" but had to find out where it started—again…not a clue.

The first opening in any investigation was finding the basement mole. As yet, he hadn't done that.

Chapter 20

Last night had been a total waste, well, maybe not a complete loss—the kids had a good time and it gave him another chance to consider asking Peterrr for some help. Peterrr had to spend the evening policing Marissa's drinking—and this did not speak well if he were going to help Chad.

"Did you get any sleep last night? You tossed and turned and kept muttering something about Indians." Sarah was clad in her pale purple bathrobe—she liked the robe but the short belt would not stay tied and she had not started her shower as yet.

Chuckling as he watched her re-tie her belt for the fifth time. "Sounds more like you're the one who didn't get any sleep." He crunched into the buttered toast and picked up his cup of coffee. "Indians, huh?"

"Yeah, I think it was Sioux Indians…at least that's what it sounded like." Finally, she managed a square knot. "There…that'll hold it."

Chad knew what she heard—it was Susame, the name of the doomsday instrument purported to be able to fry the planet or financially enslave it. "I must have been overloaded with memories of John Wayne movies." He sipped his coffee and muttered, "Why don't you go back to bed…the kids aren't up yet and I need to tie up some loose ends at the base?"

"It's a no school day, Chad…we told you that yesterday. Do you really have to go in?" Sarah knew the answer, but couldn't resist tossing out a little guilt. "Well, don't be long. I'd like to get some sun and it looks like a good day for the beach."

He nodded, "Sure…maybe a couple of hours, that's all." He pecked her cheek and chided, "Want to give the sharks another chance, huh?" With a raised arm he warded off her mock blow.

Shaking her head, she made a face as she muttered, "Bad joke, Chaddy Boy…bad joke." Sarah was sill wagging her head as she set down her coffee cup. "Have a good day."

Chad felt stumped, so the only thing he could think of was to go back to where it all began—Site C-4, the microwave station. This time he hoped to check out the "cave" area without becoming the target for a drone. "I'll give you a call when I'm done." He gave her another kiss on the cheek and whispered, "If you want to go to the beach…you better give the kids more information about your…status."

"Okay, but get out of here before the kids get up." She gave him a friendly pat on his butt and a kiss on the check. Coffee cup in hand, she headed off for the bedroom. *I doubt there's much I can say that will be a surprise,* she reminded herself.

He marveled at how she could always make him feel good—he knew she didn't want him to leave but also knew he would spend the day preoccupied if he didn't do whatever he had in mind. Mug in hand, he slipped out the side door and into his Chevrolet pickup.

Sarah glanced toward the rooms occupied by Warren and Glenda—they would be sleeping for some time yet. As Chad's truck pulled out of the driveway, she made her way to the office computer, as she had some research to continue. With Marissa in town, it looked like things might come to a head…the car "accident" had turned out to be a fortunate warning-in-waiting.

Just past Field Four he made his turn into Field Five, also known as C-4. The check points were manned like any other day, but the men on duty could not help but convey the feeling they were surprised to see him. This time he avoided the headquarters area and drove straight to the spot affectionately called "the cave." No longer considered an active crime scene, there were no APs on duty, and he scanned the sky for any rogue drones lurking about, then he got out of his truck. Chad was well aware how invisible a drone could seem, if there had been a drone, he probably would not have seen it—again he checked the sky. This time he planned to avoid using his cell.

"Good morning, Major Buford—didn't expect to see you here this morning."

Chad whirled around, knowing who he was going to see but surprised to be caught off guard--again. "What the hell are you doing here, Captain Manning? You've really got to stop sneaking up on me like that." He didn't wait for a comment, "How's Marissa's head…throbbing?"

Peterrr Manning flashed a wide smile—he resembled a TV ad for dental whitener. "You bet…she does that every once in a while. Actually, that's why I'm here…I called your house and Sarah said you were at the base. I just took a wild guess you would show up here…I was on my way here anyway." He slanted his head to one side and attempted a convincing shrug.

"Good guess."

"Well…I had to be here anyway, Major. I was here over an hour ago, waiting." He moved closer and said, "I wanted to apologize for Marissa. She's lots of fun, but sometimes she just doesn't know how to behave herself." Peterrr Manning threw up his hands, "What the hell…comes from being raised as a rich brat, I guess."

Chad considered the statement but wasn't sure what he should say. He was well aware of her background and managed to say, "Rich brat, huh? Yeah, I guess it figures!" He looked back up at the sky, "Peterrr…have you heard anything more about the two scientists that got away on the night one of them was killed?"

"Nothing solid, Chad. I'm pretty sure they made it out of here alive. Colonel Blain thinks so too." Peterrr joined in as Chad scanned the sky."You know, Major, those things are so small and can fly so high…you wouldn't see them anyway."

Chad snorted, "I'm not concerned about the ones way up there," he said, pointing to the sky, "but I'm severely concerned about the ones I can see."

"Yeah…you never really talked to us about what happened to you that day. We tried tracking you and Sarah, but, after you guys left the hospital, we couldn't find you."

"Oh, you mean after the car incident…well, you know how those things go. Somebody thought we might have been contaminated or Sarah could be developing an anurism, so they spirited us off to a closed access lab. It turned out to be no big deal, so they drugged us and then released us." He had made an effort to make his account as mundane as possible, but he doubted it really fooled Peterrr Manning.

After a few clicks of his tongue, Captain Manning broke out with a wry voice,

"Well...I'm glad it was nothing crucial. You know how rumors are around here. Some of us thought you might be working on something...special...particularly since you started checking out the fields at Eglin."

"Yeah, that's one of the things this base is famous for...rumors." Chad moved to the spot where the abductees were taken—just outside the structure called the cave. "So you never found out whose helicopter it was that picked up those two?" Chad began snooping around—the ground was of particular interest. "The first time I heard the story they said the three scientists were grabbed...kidnapped...but the tracks don't seem to bear that out. It's more like two of them were carried to this pickup spot, or two people voluntarily ran to this spot. "

"We've wondered about that too. If they 'escaped'...then we need to know *from* what or *to* what. They had some useful information about a weapons program, but I understand each man had only a piece of the puzzle—like the Michelin factories in World War Two."

Now the case was not only getting interesting but maybe, just maybe, a bit clearer. "So, if...if they left voluntarily, it is possible the one who was killed was shot to prevent an escape, not of the man but of the information." Chad made a face as he nodded, "Must be important stuff to kill one of their own people…especially the wrong person."

Peterrr made the deliberate gesture of clearing his throat."Maybe that's why they killed him, you know, useless." He finished with a reflective pause."Major…I have no doubt but what you know a hell of a lot more than you are letting on. You know this base is often working on, testing, or developing new things…so why are you trying to act so surprised?" Peterrr was pretty sure Chad would not reply but felt better having said what he did.

After a forced chuckle, Chad clasped Peterrr by the shoulder and looked into his eyes. "I'm sorry if I gave you that impression, Peterrr… I didn't mean to insult your intelligence, but at this point I don't know if it is important or not." Chad wanted to ask Peterrr if he knew bugs had been placed in Chad's house. For now, he would let it go.

Peterrr narrowed his eyes in a challenging motion."Look, Chad, I want to be perfectly clear with you. If this is the project I think it is…this is not the first time we have had this problem. The project, if we are both talking about the same thing, is so important this nation, or any other for that matter, would do whatever is necessary to develop or steal it."

Chad considered the tone of Peterrr's remarks. "Are you telling me something you're really not permitted to tell me?" He was considering the safety of his family, perhaps at this juncture even the safety of both families. "I've been here before, Captain, I am used to handling sensitive information and tracking down those who try to sell or give our secrets to other countries, corporations, or individuals." The ball was back in Peterrr's court and Chad had the feeling Peterrr was dying to tell him something—but how much?

"Counting the two we lost the other night, we have lost seven people we know of— there are others working at facilities we don't know about." He paused and moved closer to Chad and whispered, "This is not random…each of the missing persons had a different piece of the puzzle that makes up the system…Coincidence? Hardly; it is as if these escapees are trying to complete their own project before we do. In fact, 'pieces' is what they have begun calling the technicians in question.

A valuable bit of information was just given by Manning. A secret device and people "defecting" to someplace seemed more than just a possibility—perhaps even building their own Susame. *Smart plan, claim to have shut down the system while building the weapon somewhere else.* Was this a weapons race like the anxiety created in World War II or the Cold War? Who was winning? It didn't look good for our side.

"I see…because each technician is working on a different piece, they call their individual parts, 'pieces.' So who is in charge of this project, Peterrr?"

"Honestly, Chad…if there is a project,I have no idea. My guess is, like most projects, it started out private but was taken over by the government and now filtered to a government sponsored agency. All I know is it seems no one wants to talk about it and people are disappearing. We report the disappearances to the higher-ups and never hear anymore about it. I'm serious…no one wants to talk about it…at least not at staff table meetings."

"You seem concerned, Peterr, and you're talking about it." Chad tried to look into Manning's eyes but Peterrr dropped his head in resignation. "You're not *no one,* so what's your interest in this?" Chad wondered if Peterrr knew about the scientists he met with when Sarah and he were rushed off to the secret recovery hospital.

"Yeah, well, maybe I talk too much, Major. I've been known to rattle off sometimes. I just wanted to get something off my chest…you seem as safe a listener as any."

Major Buford decided to take a chance— perhaps Peterrr could point him in the right direction. "Peterr? Do you know any place on base where there is an abandoned hospital or science lab?" It was a risk, but he had to start some place…so far, things weren't going too well otherwise.

"Above or below ground?" He spoke as if he were kidding, or telling some kind of joke, but there was also a hint of seriousness in his tone.

The conversation was taking a new twist. Chad felt it best to wait out Captain

Manning's apparent willingness to confess…Chad knew too the first one to speak often loses a discussion. Something interesting was about to develop…he could feel it.

Chapter 21

Peterrr Manning sensed he was about to cross the invisible line—a point of no return of keeping a secret according to his rank and divulging what he couldn't take back. It was not a question about the man's patriotism but Chad Buford was on the prowl for something very dangerous…he could sense it—and what about the strangc happenings to Sarah and the disappearance of both he and his wife to the clandestine hospital?

"I don't know how much thought you have given it, Chad, but here in Florida we are close, very close, to Cuba, Central and South America—a haven for unstable governments, communist sympathizers and unchecked dictators." Peterrr paused to gauge Chad's attention—he was interested.

Their conversations were taking on the similarity of a chess game or a tennis match.After gesturing with a short nod, Chad said, "You're right…I know about all of that, but really haven't given it that much thought." He waited, "Is this geo-political lesson going somewhere?" He tipped his head and smiled.

"Damned straight, Chad…I just wanted to prepare you for the answer you are about to get concerning abandoned facilities." Peterrr looked around—he pursed his lips and sighed, "Feel like a cup of coffee?"

"Why? Do I look like one?" Chad laughed and put out his hand, "Be glad to buy you one…at some place with lots of background noise."

The captain bobbed his head and pointed at his car, "I've got an oversized thermos in my car and we can drive to Duke Field (Field Three)—the 919th or the 728th Tactical should be making lots of noise at this time of day." Peterrr turned to start walking to his car, but noticed Chad's hesitation. "I'll be the first to drink from my thermos, Major…and we can talk at some spot…out side my car…your choice." He began walking, "…and we can frisk each other…if you're feeling the necessity for such action." Peterrr laughed. "Let's go—"

After pulling out on Highway 85, the silent duo went north, past the east gate—and the twelve miles north to Field Three passed quickly. "Ever been to Field Two, Major?" After passing the guard post, Peterrr took a left turn that became a hard packed sand driveway (special wide-tires suggested).

"Sure, a couple of times…why?" Chad didn't like talking in the car…it could be bugged or Peterrr could have a recorder or transmitter any place in his body. "Is that part of the tour?"

"How about here…this is a good place to watch the crews take off and land. Doing touch and goes today—it's kind of deafening, but I find it rather stimulating." He raised his voice to a shout as two jets passed overhead.

They left the car and took the thermos of hot coffee with them. Another pair of jets screamed by and ignited their after burners—the sound was earsplitting. Normally, this locale would not be a good place to install a listening device…the jet noise would shatter most pickup devices.

As Peterrr began pouring coffee he hushed his voice and began talking like a tour guide. "In 1975 Base Two was a Vietnamese Resettlement Camp. Not all of those being 'resettled' were happy about staying at the camp, as one would expect." He looked up and began putting coffee in Chad's cup. "Rumor has it, 'and you know how rumors are,' they built a few tunnels…and a few underground structures. The water table doesn't really permit underground housing in every part of this peninsula." Casually, he continued, "Some say the Bay of Pigs fiasco was planned and launched from right here."

Chad watched as Peterrr took a deep sip from his plastic cup. "You think there are some uncharted or empty facilities on Field Three?" He sipped his coffee—it was hot, almost the color of printer ink and strong. He watched as Peterrr nodded his head. "I know you're hinting at something…let me guess." With his free hand he made a sweeping gesture, "It's possible there are folks working clandestine government projects…or possibly for governments not friendly to the U. S., even Latin American dictators, or they may have friends connected to a shadow U. S. Government program."

Tipping his eyes upward, Peterrr rolled his head to the side and pushed his lips together—like it pained him to answer the statement. "I'd say it is about how I see it." He moved closer to Chad, "There is something going on at this base…something big, something above my pay grade to get any advanced Intel. I get the feeling it's as big as the Manhattan Project was for our first atomic test at Alamogordo—that kind of fervor."

It was strange to hear this man tell him his hunch and under any other circumstances he would consider it a breach of security. Chad had to weigh the words he was hearing. Maybe Peterrr was right—some of the Latin American countries were beholding to nations like Russia, China, Iran and North Korea—anyone with money and power willing to screw the other guy. "So where do you suggest I begin looking?"

"I'd suggest *we* begin looking inside any of the deserted hangers or buildings on Field Two, at least it's a start." Peterrr tossed down the last of his cup of coffee. "Want some more?"

"Sure." This was an interesting development. Was Captain Peterrr Manning really interested in helping him look for the missing scientists and subsequently a shadow team of weapons or benign energy developers or just trying to stay close so he could keep an eye on the Major's progress? "Why do you want to be in on the search?"

"It's on *my* base too, Chad. I know you're sort of an independent 'hot shot' civilian, but you are still a Major in the reserves. I figure if you smell out something that could be a detriment to this base and our country…well, I should be involved. That's about as plain as I can put it." He looked up as he finished popping the stopper in his thermos. "I'm hoping you see it the same way. We both work to keep the base secure."

"Okay, fellow 'hot shot,' what are *we* looking for?" Chad was pretty sure Peterrr had no idea about the Susame Project or where the missing scientists were hiding but, then, like every other person, he had been wrong before.

"You tell *me*. All I know is what my gut tells me…you're into something big and I want to be involved…call it a lust for adventure, maybe a thirst for advancement, or perhaps I've been bitten by the patriotic bug." Peterrr gave out a muted chuckle and breathlessly said, "I always liked Indiana Jones."

Chad knew what his decision would be, but he went through a series of facial gestures intended to display a level of concern. "Okay, but I can't tell you very much yet…let's see how it goes first. We'll start out 'inspecting' the hangers and then move on to the other buildings." He glanced at his watch, and snorted, "Let's hope we don't find *The Temple of Doom*. Right now I am really late…I promised Sarah I'd be back home after a couple of hours. She knows I won't, but I promised to take the kids to the beach so she could get some sunshine." Chad wondered, *why would anyone want to make a weapon that had the potential of destroying the planet by misusing the earth's magnetic field as weapon? What would be left for the bad guys to reap? Why do it?*

Peterrr looked at Chad as if he were reading his mind, "You look worried, major." Peterrr was reading a grave, guarded expression frightening to see, the heaviness a person displays when a precious member of his family is in mortal danger. "How are Sarah and the baby doing? Are Warren and Glenda okay?" He wasn't just prying, he had a genuine concern.

Quickly, Chad changed his expression, "They're all fine, Peterr." He hesitated, then said, "Nope, just some things I need to get done." The same question kept torchering his mind; *would a bunch of power happy fanatics really build a weapon that could fry mankind quicker than a flame-thrower?* He wondered. He could picture his family playing at the beach and suddenly…a ray of light touches them something no one could see—who sees magnetism, only the results, and poof--they are vaporized…just like that.

"Look, Chad, Marissa and I might see you at the beach, Marissa's friend is staying at a motel for a few days, and we are obligated to show her and her boyfriend the sights."

It was a relief to have something, anything, break into his thoughts of eminent disaster. "I'm sure Warren and Glenda would be happy to see Carl and Betsy…I'll tell Sarah." His thoughts flashed back to possible fears…too much time around Marissa was inviting troubles—he recalled a friend who once told him 'He never met a worry he didn't like.' Chad shook it off and put the thought back in his memory bank. "Peterrr, you realize if we go down this road, our families might be in jeopardy?"

"What are you talking about?" Peterrr said, not kidding. "In our line of work, that's the way it always is and always was."

Chad rubbed his face with his palm and sighed, "Yeah, you're right, but I've got a real bad feeling in my gut about this one." He chucked Peterrr in the arm and said, "See you later, 'Indiana.' Thanks."

Chapter 22

The drug world had probably been his main business all his life—cheap to obtain, easy to distribute and always an army of stupid addicts willing to pay outrageous money to screw up their brains. Hector Rodrigo was proud of being the third generation to run the "family business"— both his father and grandfather had been gunned down by rival gangs, perhaps by Hector himself if the buzz were right.

For the last thirty days he had been putting loose ends together in order to be ready for the follow-up meeting with Miracle Chu. He was still angry about the mess one of his men had made while trailing a truck following Sarah Buford. For his incompetence his body was now at the bottom of the Gulf of Mexico.

With a broad wave of his arm, he signaled his young daughter to step closer to him—he stiffened as he watched her tense up and pan the room…she used to do that when her mother was alive. "Come here, Little One, Daddy wants to talk to you."

. She would soon be nineteen and her pretend boyfriend would still not leave her alone. "I don't feel well today, Daddy."

He sounded sympatric but she knew he was like a filthy animal in a human body—just like her boyfriend. if her plan worked out she would be able to escape from both of them…and soon. "Come…come here," he said, "I have some good news to tell you."

Again she looked around the room—they were alone, deathly alone. With slow, short steps, she moved closer to the evil man. "I really don't feel good today, Daddy." Hector had a reputation of likeing to compromise younger girls---she wanted no part of it.

A wave of anger welled up in Hector Rodrigo. He was a man not used to people ignoring his orders, but he needed her. At least as part of his plan for his visitors…yes, at least for a little while longer. His fingers locked onto her forearm—like an anaconda cutting off all feeling in her fingers. He liked the feeling of power and displayed his control every chance he got. "Look into my eyes, Little One." He seldom used her real name—the very sight of her was beginning to remind him of her rebellious stepmother and that the name 'Little One' was getting too old for his taste and she continued to resist his unwanted attentions.

Little One looked into his smoldering eyes and listened to his lying words, "You know how much I love you—you mean the world to me. When I look at your beauty, you remind me of your sainted mother, My Child." He relaxed his grip and studied her…she was indeed getting too old, and too wise, for him and he would soon replace her with a younger, more compliant girl. "I have a friend, who is coming to visit. I'm sure you will remember him. I want you to be especially nice to him while he is visiting. It is very important to our family. Do you understand me?" He forced a cajoling smile but he meant every word.

Inside, she winced. She knew what was coming—his friends were just as evil as he. "Yes, Daddy, I understand…I'll be nice to him." *If I'm still around…you sick pervert.* She would say anything to free her arm and get out of the room without being "his good girl," as he so often said.

"Good…good, yes, that will be good." *Yes, she was being too resistant and maybe he would give her to Chu…the old codger might like that,* he thought.

He patted the back of her hand and released his grip, "Now, run along and play with your friends. We'll talk later." He watched as she dashed across the room, her small shoes tapping on the terrazzo floor. Hector didn't think of himself as a pervert, an evil man of tyrannical moods, rather as a benefactor keeping the girl from living in the slums of Caracas. Her "performed duties" were just a reward for time well spent, an expression of gratitude—that's how he preferred to think of the matter. After all, father time was about to catch up with Hector.

* * *

The sleek Gulfstream V touched down on a remote landing strip on the outskirts of Caracas and Hector nudged his bodyguard, "It's hard to believe this old man is still alive…he has survived at least ten death attempts."

Smugly, the six foot six bodyguard snickered, "Must have a good bodyguard, don't you think?" Hector didn't respond. Proudly, the bodyguard reached inside his tropical weight suit jacket and adjusted one of his three pistols. "Or he's lucky as hell."

Hector studied the walk of Miracle Chu—it was a proud stride, tempered by the humility of seventy-three years of life. "They don't call him 'Miracle' for nothing." It was a few words spoken without separating Hector's lips. After a deep, calming breath, Hector began his walk to meet the elderly man.

Miracle and Hector embraced—as was the custom for people in the business who distrusted each other. For Chu, this venture was strictly business—a chance to increase his slice of the world's money and power. At his age, while he was not ready to die, he wanted to leave a legacy worthy of all the misery he had created. "Mister Rodrigo…apparently this climate agrees with you…you remember my son, Ronald—"

For some reason, Hector thought the man behind Miracle was just one of his man-servants—perhaps it was nothing more than the way the twenty-three-year-old walked in the old man's shadow. Hector knew the young man was perfectly fluent in Spanish, but he chose to address him in English. "I'm pleased to see you again, Ronald, …you've certainly grown into a very handsome young man, I must say." After a polite smile and handshake, Hector stepped next to Miracle.

The elderly CBA (Chinese-born American) grabbed Ronald's arm, "He just graduated from MIT—Massachusetts Institute of Technology, Hector. He did it in just a little over two years. He's a smart boy…don't know where he got it, but his mother used to take the credit." There was an observable wistfulness anytime he spoke of his recently departed wife, as she had been his constant friend and, often, his moral advisor. "His mother would have been very proud."

For a brief time the two men walked side by side until they left the tarmac and entered the relative safety of Hector's bulletproof limousine. Caracas was the assassination capital of the world, a commonplace event as drug lords walked from their airplanes and hotels to cars.

Hector was more than aware of Ronald's brilliance—it was Ronald who first brought to their attention the energy and climate control prospects of the Susame Project, though not a face-to-face meeting. The concept was simple—use magnetism to selectively interrupt the earth's protective belt. Lanthanide elements were being suggested because of their ability to align and result in a strong magnetic field, workable but pricy. Hector disliked the young man for his brilliance, money and youthful good looks, but most of all…his unearned power. Simply, the kid hadn't yet put in his time. Unlike Hector and Miracle, the kid had not yet gotten his hands dirty…his father had kept him out of that end of the business.

Once inside the limousine, the body guards in place, the three men settled into small talk—Ronald sat in the seat facing his father and Mister Rodrigo.

"I hear you made contact with the team in Florida, Hector. Were the negotiations fruitful?" Miracle leaned forward and accepted a glass of water from Ronald. Miracle probed for an answer. "Some of our investors are quite concerned that project expenses may be mismanaged. There are also those grumbling about the direction the project has taken." He sipped his water and continued, waving his hand, "You have any thoughts about this, Hector?"

"Of course I share your concern…no one wants to see our profits squandered, Mister Chu. However, I want to assure you that…" He nodded as he took a tumbler of Scotch on the rocks from Ronald. "…we have a group of our best people watching every penny."

Ronald laced his fingers together and leaned closer to Hector—Ronald could feel his own disgust beginning to stir but kept it in check and smiled. His secret letters to

Victoria Rodrigo told him all he needed to know about this excuse for a man. "We believe you, Mister Rodrigo."

"Please, call me Hector." The drug lord formed an insincere smile.

The young man looked at his father, Miracle Chu. "Mister Rodrigo…" He deliberately did not accept the familiarity of 'Hector'. "The governments which are involved realize this project will run into the nine digit range, and they are willing to pay the money."

Ronald shifted his attention to Hector. "But…they also realize with numbers that large there is a tendency to …shall we say, misplace some of the funds." Ronald sat back and watched the smoldering eyes of the Latin American.

The inference was very clear,someone had accused Hector of embezzlment…probably the nuisance,"Barnacle." It was no secret they were having a problem—drug sales were not going as well as they had hoped. Local politicians wanted to curry the favor of the United States and thereby receive certain funds which would be at their personal disposal for doing so. Crop fields had been burned and arrests had been made.

"It is true that a few gnats are bothering our business but we are not using Sun funds to make up for the shortfall." He was noticeably nervous as he took a gulp from his drink and waiting for the response to his shallow retort.

"We're very pleased to hear that, Hector. Of course we were not concerned, but you know how tongues wag in this business." Miracle patted Hector on the knee and smiled at Ronald, "See…I told you— all we had to do was to talk the situation through and arrive at some kind of consensus."

"Yes, Father, I can see the wisdom of your patience." Ronald could tell his father did not believe Hector…and was also certain Hector knew as much. For the rest of their visit they would have to be particularly careful to avoid any unforeseen "accidents."

They approached the driveway that weaved its way up a steep hill toward Hector's mansion…

Ronald took a steadying breath…and thought of only one word, *Victoria.*

Chapter 23

His heart pounded against his ribs—he heard every thump in his blood reddened ears. Little One stood in front of him and Ronald could not touch her—he wanted to take her in his arms and claim her for his own. The pain was agonizing as he caught himself staring into her dazzling blue eyes. "Hello, Victoria…it's good to see you again. I must tell you of my latest trip to the States."

From the first time the two had met, Victoria had fallen in love with the young, thin, boy of nineteen. She was just short of her fifteenth birthday at the time, but her time with Hector had made her wise well beyond her calendar years—at least she knew a good person when she met one.

Ronald was only half Chinese—the result of a marriage by Miracle to a much younger Spanish girl who was attending a university in the United States—Miracle had been a guest lecturer and tutor. Their marriage was a happy one that lasted twenty-five years— until four years before she died from complications of common flu. Just after his mother's death, Ronald met Victoria…her gentleness helped him through a turbulent time. Their correspondence had not only preserved their friendship but caused it to blossom into something entirely unexpected—love.

Victoria rose, popping up on her tiptoes and diplomatically kissed Ronald on the cheek. She felt his body shudder from her touch—his cheeks turned a bright red against his olive complexion. "Why, Ronald, you're blushing!" she whispered in his ear. Even across the room Little One could feel the burning jealousy of Hector Rodrigo's stare. She hooked onto Ronald's arm. "So…tell me about America". She deliberately called the United States"America" because it made Hector angry.

"This is America. The other place is North America…why can't you get it straight? I should never have agreed to your North American studies!" Then Hector would go into a rant about the United States of America, and so it went.

Sheepishly, Ronald walked with Victoria while she took him to the massive patio that was surrounded on three sides by part of Hector's villa. One side had a low wall that allowed an unobstructed view of the valley below. Victoria had a genuine interest in all things from "the States," recently learning she had been born to an American girl, a little over nineteen years ago. From Hector's private files she gathered he had "adopted" her from an agency that specialized in children of unwed mothers from wealthy families. The files said her mother had a short, but sincere affair with a young American. The child was ripped out of the mother's arms and spirited off to the agency that sold her to Hector.

Hector had paid the boarding school to take care of her until she was six years old, then he brought her to Caracas, Venezuela. Her stepmother was kind to her and was able to restrain Hector until Victoria (as she called her) was nine years old. Shortly after the disagreement, the stepmother met with a well planned, fatal accident.

Victoria moved her head and gestured with her arms as if giving her "friend" a thorough tour of the garden. The words coming out of her mouth were different. "Ronald, I can't stand being so close to you and not being able to kiss every inch of your body." She calmed down a bit and added, "You've changed a lot in the last few years…taller, even more handsome. You even look more Spanish. Will you be here long?"

He stopped and bent down to more closely examine an exotic plant. His fingers caressed the pistils of the plant as he thought of Victoria. "Funny how much this flower reminds me of you…you need the name of a pretty flower." Ronald stood up straight, "I don't know—it depends on when my father and Hector complete their discussions. My father does not trust any business not discussed in face-to-face talks."

She knew that Hector was probably watching them…if not directly, then on one of the surveillance cameras. "Hector seems unusually nervous…for days he has been on edge—snapping at everything. He has even killed several of his business partners." Stopping, she turned to face Ronald and said, "Do you know what all of this is about?" Coyly, she added, "I listen to his phone calls and read his e-mails… I know more than he thinks."

Ronald knew what she was hopping. She was anticipating someone would kill Hector or have him killed, but he was a powerful man and it would have to be someone like Miracle who did it. "I wouldn't get my hopes up just yet…they have a project that requires Hector's connections in the United States. I'm not sure what that is, but it's probably temporary at best." He was hiding the truth from her. Ronald had attended a scientific convention and heard a presentation on the possibility of harnessing the sun's power or duplicating its make-up as a more useful energy source, something the world would become dependent on…and they would see to it. The aspiration would be to replace electricity and fossil fuels, maybe even control the earth's climates…it was Ronald who encouraged his father to get involved. Abruptly, Ronald looked up at the sky, "When will I be able to see you?"

The meaning was clear, and it sent tremors though her young body."It's difficult…we have to be patient. I love you, Ronald, and my life here is agonizing, every day agonizing when I cannot see you. Help me…PLEASE." She squeezed his hand as if sending him a clandestine message.

Hector and Miracle sat by the garden pool on the west side of the mansion Hector acquired from a previous business partner. Already the sun's late rays cast a pinkish-gold light transforming everything into a fairyland. The ultimate effect was peace and love…an ironic absurdity in light of these maniacal monsters of drug land.

For Victoria, the long walk back to her room was a new kind of torture. With every step she seemed to move further away from the man with whom she wanted to spend every waking moment. There were things she needed to tell him…things Hector did not know she had heard by grapevine. Hector's obsession with this Susame thing was preoccupying him to the point he was neglecting his drug business…and it was increasingly evident he had no intention of sharing its power with anyone. She was surprised that Miracle and Ronald would be involved in the development of such a questionable undertaking when the outcome seemed predetermined.

Miracle listened politely to Hector's constant raving about his problems with politicians. He was listening with only *half an ear*—Hector seemed to think because Miracle's wife was Spanish he was interested in the affairs of South and Central America. He nodded politely, but continued to consider the implications of Ronald's reaction to Victoria. "I'm sure all of this will be straightened out as soon as the elections in the United States are over…Barnacle has assured me."

"Barnacle? Huh! I hope so. I'm sure you're right, Miracle…'cuz if that isn't so I'm going to have to deal with a couple of our politicians."

The two men shifted their attention to Ronald as he approached. "Hector, this is even more beautiful than your other mansion." Ronald cast his eyes about the landscaping, the view and the inspiring sunset. "Exquisite."

"Are you talking about my humble patio, or my Little One?" The words were delivered as if by a friendly father asking about his intentions toward his daughter—he smiled, but the words seemed to have a certain edge. "She's quite lovely, don't you agree?"

Miracle was annoyed by the bluntness of Hector's comments…he turned his head and glared at his host. "What do you mean? The boy has been friends with your…your daughter for some time."

"That's okay, father… I'm sure Hector did not mean anything improper. We both appreciate the fine young woman she has become." He tipped his head as if to study the crafty drug lord. "Is that not right, Hector?" Ronald reached into a bowl of mixed nuts and casually grabbed a handful.

A small flock of birds took flight as Hector boomed out in laughter. "Your son has an excellent grasp of things, Mister Chu." Recovering from the forced outburst, Hector painted on a smile that imitated a self-conscious teenager. "I am honored you appreciate her…she has grown into a delicate young lady, not Spanish mind you, but still superb in every way."

There was an obvious tension in the air and Miracle knew he would have to deal with this issue, but at a later time. "Hector? What have you heard from our friends in the States? I am getting a lot of pressure from business partners on the mainland."

"Only from Florida…Barnacle says almost everything is being funneled though the team at the Air Force base. A trial test is scheduled within a couple of weeks, maybe sooner…but I must tell you they are under a great deal of scrutiny."

"From whom?" Miracle did not like the tone of Hector's report—it was hesitant and filled with contingencies. "What is being done? Surely, there are those who will resist the impact this will have on the global economy, but the need is crucial."

Hector's skin almost turned white as he realized the depth of Miracle's concern. "There is a certain major getting rather nosey…an officer now in the reserves. He is a good intelligence officer and has begun to search the base for information…Barnacle is concerned and I think with reason."

Ronald shoved some more nuts into his mouth, "Bribe, blackmail, or butcher…which one of the B's would you like to use?" Ronald was much more of a scientist than a criminal-businessman but understood the ways drug dealers dealt with problems…particularly Hector. "This is a simple decision, is it not? We must do what is in the best interest of the project and our partners." He paused to make sure he had not overstepped his bounds…Miracle nodded. He had only said what Hector would want to hear.

"If we kill him, will that hurt or help our timetable?" Miracle paused, "What does Barnacle say?" It was a probative question—was Hector pursuing the line of weapons development, as Miracle suspected, or was he talking about energy production?

"Barnacle thinks a discreet death might be possible, but the major has acquired a captain who is showing some interest…but we are certain we know how to deal with him. His wife might put him in a precarious position." Hector narrowed his eyes as he thought, "We can stop him…that is the important point, I would think. It is just that I'm not sure we can control some of our American partners if we start killing off two officers or their families. Do you see the dilemma?"

"So, the captain is containable…but the major may have to be eliminated?" Ronald summarized the discussion. "Of course we are talking some kind of accident…are we not?"

Miracle made a face that replicated the famous yellow "sad face"—the corners of his mouth dropped and the chin moved forward. "I don't like it." He began shaking his head in little, rapid movements. "This Major… Major Buford, I believe is his name, has a good reputation for surviving death attempts. Then there is the problem of the Captain… This man, Manning, just might respond in a more zealous way." He looked up as if seeking inspirations—"We should strike at their weak points…their wives and children, not deaths…just leverage. With the test this close…we should not jeopardize our position and incur any unwanted sideways flack. When the world sees the benefit of Susame, they should overlook most anything, don't you think?"

A scowl shot across Ronald's face, "Father, surely you don't mean to harm the wives or the children?"

Responding with a face that displayed confusion, Miracle said, "Son, how could you think that. If the family is dead…they would no longer be of any use to us." Miracle was now convinced that Hector and Barnacle were behind the shift to weapons development. That conclusion was inescapable.

"I don't understand your concern, Ronald." Hector interjected. "You said yourself we need to protect the project and investors. Is that not so?"

"Gentlemen, may I suggest another approach. We know of several nations that would like to develop the Susame beam but just can't put together the funds. Also, we should have a test model soon…a successful test model." Miracle paused to see if they were following his line of reasoning.

"Okay, Ronald, you are right, but I don't see what that has to do with our problem." Hector was being polite not to upset the son of a powerful partner.

"Okay, then, I would like to suggest we send them on a number of harmless 'wild goose chases,'" Ronald said. "Feed information about some of the other people who have already failed. By the time they realize they have been tricked…it will be too late." Ronald looked at Miracle to see if his father approved of the safer course of action…he didn't care about what Hector thought.

Miracle gently massaged his miniature goatee, his eyes blinking rapidly. "Yes, my Son, that could be most useful, but…I propose we do *both.* " He held up his fingers, "First we start a campaign of disinformation…<u>and</u> we put in place a few warnings…make them feel as if they are making progress."

"Won't that defeat our purpose, father?"

"Not if we make it appear the threats are coming from the people that we are using to distract them." Miracle smiled and went on, "You see…they will go after them because they threatened their families…AND because they will want to defeat their attempts to beat the United States at developing the Susame beams." Miracle closed his eyes and nodded with self approval, "Barnacle will see to it."

The three men nodded in agreement.

"Now, Mister Rodrigo, we are back to money. Let's have a look at your accounts…about which my associates have asked me to inquire. I need to be prepared for my meeting with Barnacle." Miracle stood up and turned to his son, "Of course you will join us, Son…I think we shall need your assistance."

Hector gave a wide smile…inside, his intestines were convulsing. His accounts were clever, but were they clever enough? Probably not. A feeling of weakness was beginning to work its way though his muscles. *I should never have agreed to become involved in this expensive mess,* he thought. *Now it's going to bite me in the ass.* Some investors expected a global renaissance to help mankind …others demanded a powerful weapon to be used to take over the planet. To some…they were the same.

Chapter 24

For Captain Peterrr Manning, the past ten days had been nothing but hell. Digging into old records and scouting out deserted buildings were not his idea of a "good duty station." Major Buford would not tell him everything, but he could tell by the emphasis given to the search this was something really important—besides, it could help Peterrr's career, so that was good enough for him. To top it off, Marissa had been getting threats—mainly targeted at the children…her most vulnerable spot.

"You won't be…be gone so long… today, will you, Peterrr?" Marissa was wringing her hands and interjecting words in between shallow sobs. With a rapid movement of her arm, she sloshed some vodka into a wide-mouthed shot glass.

Peterrr moved to comfort her, as he had never seen her like this…something about these messages were really getting to her.

He had thought the visit by her girlfriend would help but only seemed to make things worse. What bothered him most was that she refused to discuss the matter with him—all she would say was, 'Stay out of it!'

"I'll be back just as soon as I can…we have to finish our tour of Field Two and it's just turned out to be more complicated than we had thought, Marissa. There are a ton of leads we need to follow up…and there may not be a lot of time, Mar."

"I don't give a damn about your pretending to be some kind of super sleuths, but I think you should care as much about your family." She stamped her foot on the tile floor and spilled her drink, "Ever since you two started digging around, you have spent more time with that stupid Major than with us." She moved to a bar stool and began to cry. "I need you *here!*"

Peterrr moved closer to her and tried to lift up her sagging head, but she only shook him off. "I'll be back…soon." He turned and made his way out of the door. It was not easy to leave her like that, but he knew even if he spent the entire day in her presence she would still be drinking and ranting all day long…he had to get away before he said something he would regret.

In the quiet of the car, he could not avoid thinking about this sudden bout of misery and despair…and could not shake the feeling there must be something ominous about the phone calls. Whether past or present he could not tell.

Peterrr's mind snapped back to reality when he saw Chad waiting by his car, leaning over the hood and studying a map. "What's new today?"

Chad could sense the unsteadiness in the voice of his associate."Marissa still giving you trouble?" Chad considered telling Peterrr about the calls Sarah had been getting but decided it would be better to let the ladies work it out…besides, it was possible they had nothing to do with each other. Still…it seemed someone didn't like what they were doing. Threats usually meant they were getting close.

"Yeah, but this time it was an e-mail that popped up on her computer. Just the same old generic threats…I think it's some kind of prank, but, hey, how the hell should I know. She never really tells me anything."

With an understanding nod, Chad pointed to a spot on the map. "Yesterday I did a bit of digging in some of the old engineering files. Look here… this blueprint seemed to come out of nowhere and shows there was once a hospital and research lab at this spot. I checked all the orders for demolition and there is no record of it actually being destroyed, but…" he pointed to a sandy meadow in front of them, "…you can see there is nothing down there." The ground was dotted with clumps of struggling grass and pocked with discarded cans, bottles and empty cold medicine boxes.

"So you think it was underground, or someone just didn't record they covered it up." Peterrr pursed his lips and whistled, "Maybe it's what we're looking for…did you call for some police back up?"

"I don't think that's a good idea, Peterr, too many loose lips on this base and this thing we're checking into is beyond top secret."

Peterrr could not help but make a subtle comparison—Chad would not tell him anything and neither would Marissa… It seemed no one trusted him. "Top Secret, huh, so when do you plan on giving me a clue so I can contribute to this witch hunt?"

The words just fell out of his mouth and with more force than he would have liked. "I know…I know…I invited myself on this thing… Let's get busy."

Ignoring the outburst, Chad returned to the map and pointed at the spot where they would start searching. "I brought a little helper with us today."

Peterrr followed Chad to the back of the Hum-V and watched as Chad opened the back doors. In front of him was a device which looked a lot like the treasure seeking devices he had seen at the beach. "We're looking for gold or coins?"

Chad smiled. He then lifted the device out of the truck. "This little baby may look like a common Zircon MT6 metal detector but I assure you it can look into the earth for at least thirty feet and feed back a picture of anything between that depth and the surface."

"I saw something like that on one of those CSI movies…they were looking for bodies." Peterrr nodded his approval.

"It would be faster if we split up, but I think it will be safer if we stick together. One of us will mark on the map where we have checked and one of us will operate the machine…we can take turns. With any luck we can be done here and then move to another area."

Chad turned on the device and moved a couple of dials…a picture of airplane parts appeared on the small screen. We can adjust the width of the picture…how about let's start with a wide sweep?"

Slowly they moved over the designated area—most of the underground revealed old refueling tanks, septic tanks, and miscellaneous trash which must have been left when it was a Vietnamese Relocation Center. Airplane parts and some ancient anti aircraft guns had been plowed under when the camp no longer served a purpose.

"Sure is a lot of crap underground. So what we are looking for is an area someone could still use as a laboratory or for…'something,' right?"

"You got it, Slick, I don't know where it is, Peterr, but I'll know what's happening. For simplicity's sake, I think we should move to center grid and work our way out to the northwest corner." Chad smiled and began to walk to the spot designated on his map.

For three hours they patiently walked over the land—sweeping back and forth in an effort to examine what was under the surface. Fortunately, they weren't searching for something small, items as large as a filing cabinet, a stainless steel table or, better yet, some laboratory equipment. They were just considering taking a break, when Peterrr slowed down and then stopped.

"Chad!" he whispered, "Look at this…what do you think it is?" Peterrr moved his face so he could get a clearer picture from the monitor. "Looks like a bunch of …conveyor belts, or long tables, maybe even a metal floor."

Impressed with their luck, Chad felt a bit nervous—if they had really found something of importance, perhaps someone was watching them. Quickly he glanced in all directions. "Peterrr…do you have the feeling we're being watched?"

"I don't know…could be some of the APs are curious." He pointed at the screen, "So, what do you think?"

"Looks promising, but is it accessible, or just covered with dirt?" He grabbed the detector and made some adjustments. "Wow…it's open down there, Peterr… It shows open!" Now Chad started scanning the ground as he looked for an opening—a set of stairs, an elevator, a cave entrance,,, anything. "He followed the readings in every direction until he came to a spot where the top view looked like a metal door suspended by a track. "I think that's a door to this place."

"I'm with you, but where does it come out?" Peterrr pointed at a line on the screen, "Is that a metal hand rail?" Chad nodded in uncertainty.

Silently, the two men tracked the thin line as it moved toward an area consisting of deserted airplane hangars—the line was now becoming larger and clearer.

"What do you think; Peterrr? Bet the access is in one of those old buildings." Chad picked up the pace and began to jog in the direction of one old building in particular. He started talking quickly and in short breaths, "Some of these…hangers still…have…aircraft in them."

Chapter 25

Both men were sure they were on to something. "Yeah, but most…are old ones…that are kept…for the parts…or for some joker trying…to restore one…so he can rent it…to the movie people." Peterrr's words were breaking up as they made a turn that took them to the back of the hanger. It looked as if it had been vandalized by some kids. Windows were broken out, and glass was scattered about the cracked, oil stained, concrete floor. Wild grass and plants had taken over some of the cracks.

Chad gasped as he leaned forward and rested his hands on his knees, "Looks like a great place for some homeless snakes or gators… Be careful and move slowly, Peterr."

Peterrr Manning shuttered, "Damn right! I hate both of those critters and don't think they like me either." He pulled out his service weapon, intending to use it, if necessary.

"I don't think that's a good idea, Peterr. There may be homeless people here…and they might not want any visitors. Maybe even a gas leak or two in a place like this could…well, you know." Chad stopped and glanced up at the sky. "Have you seen anything of a drone or any surveillance cameras?" Instinctively, Chad checked his own Glock 9 mm, like a tranquilizer, it helped to settle his nerves.

Putting away his pistol, Peterrr looked about the inside of the hanger—it was small as hangers go…probably built for single engine trainer planes. "Surveillance cameras? I don't know, Chad…there's too much crap in this place to tell. With all this junk you could hide a small tank."

"Okay…let's check it out. You take that wall and I'll take this one." Chad paused and gave Peterrr a mock salute, "And, Captain…stay in sight. We don't want any more mysterious disappearances."

A wry smile passed over Peterrr's lips as he returned the salute, "Don't worry about me, Major… I'm the very sole wit of caution. But…I do wish you would give me an idea what I'm looking for."

"Ah, yes…well, for now, just find an entrance to the underground place. It might turn out to be nothing, Peterr, but on the other hand we might find a nest of vipers…the two-legged kind.

Walking inside the deserted hanger was like being in another world. The frequent rains had deposited scattered pools of water—most of them reflecting rainbows of oil floating on the surface. Every step cast a plaintive echo muffled by the scattered pieces of office equipment and machinery which had once been shiny and new. Chad had the feeling he was in a dream, walking about in a war memorial mausoleum of things that once served their purpose, now discarded like old people retired to Florida. He glanced over at Peterrr Manning and thought, *When is it our turn?* Quickly, he snapped out of the unfruitful path of depression, "Peterr…you see anything over there? For chrissakes, I can't find anything."

"Na, just a lot of rust and mold," he said. Holding his breath, he stepped around a spot where something had used the hanger floor as a toilet. "Watch your step around some of this mess!"

"Yeah, I found some of that crap too. Let's stay in view of each other and then we can check out the offices." Chad could not help thinking about how there should have been an echo in such a large place and further reasoned to himself, *Too open to the outside and too full of junk…*

Time just seemed to drift away, like a plastic bottle floating in the Pacific Ocean it was going somewhere, but the destination was labeled 'unknown.' The two explorers moved about, turning over junk that reminded them of searching the ocean floor or rummaging through the remains of an ancient sea vessel.

To Peterrr's right side was a wall of metal lockers—at one time they must have been slate gray, shiny and labeled with names, but now they were pitted and edged in rust. He almost walked past the grouping when suddenly he stopped…something was inconsistent, but he couldn't place what it was. "Chad…I think I've found something, can you give me a hand?"

It only took Chad a few seconds to cross to the other side of the building. His heart beat fast from the prospect of discovery. Breathlessly, he asked Peterrr, "What did you find?"

"Lockers…Two of them." Peterrr Manning took two steps back and stood next to Chad Buford. "Look at the doors."

At first, everything looked just as it should—the doors were all in a line…closed and decorated with faded labels. "They look like any other locker doors that I've seen, Peterr. So what's the problem?" Chad frowned and his ego was a bit bruised by the thought Peterrr was seeing something he wasn't.

Instead of answering, Peterrr stepped forward and grabbed the handle of one of the locker doors. "These three doors don't look as abused as the others…like they have never been opened, Chad."Cautiously, Chad moved up close to the metal doors. "I see what you mean." Chad grinned, "So you wonder what's behind door number three, huh?"

Peterr started to pull on the door.

"NO…NO, don't do that!" He watched as Peterr froze in his tracks. Chad lowered his voice and said, "It might be booby trapped."

"Oh, yeah…I've heard of that but would it still work after so many years?" Peterr stepped back from the door as if it were an attacking alligator. He looked at Chad. In unison, the two men said, "I don't want to find out." The moment of laughter helped to relieve the tension but both were alive with the prospect they might have found an entrance to the ground below.

Peterr quipped, "What would Indian Jones do?"

"Probably get us both killed!" was Chad's answer. "Let's check it…"

The ringing of a cell phone resounded like the explosion of a stick of dynamite. After a quick jerk and flash of adrenalin, Peterr grabbed his phone from the case hanging on his belt. "Yeah?" He listened and then mouthed, "Marissa."

While Peterr moved a few yards away, Chad began examining the structure of the wall of lockers—thirteen of them, all mounted up from the floor and resting on a concrete pad six inches thick. He shot a look to Peterr…it didn't take long to realize he was having a heated discussion with Marissa about something.

Upon closer examination, he saw the locker doors number nine and ten were joined together as well as locker doors number eleven and twelve. *So there are four doors involved*, he told himself. Chad guessed each set was suspended on the inside by a large set of hinges which allowed each set to open and form a large opening four doors in width. *Clever! But why?*

"She's been drinking again." Peterr rolled his eyes and said, "Look, Chad, I'm going to have to leave pretty soon. I don't want the kids to come home and find her like that. For now, they are playing at Hillary's…with 'Uncle Blainy.'" He took a deep breath and sighed, "She says she got another call, but it was different. This time the person asked for me before he jumped on her." He glanced at the lockers and asked Chad, "Find out anything?" It was obvious he wanted to drop the Marissa subject.

Quickly, Chad showed him what he had found and what he thought it meant. "I think, if we opened these four doors, we would find an entrance to the lower level. It's not all that secretive, but it would keep the casual eye from spotting the existence of whatever they were doing below. It might even lead to a safety bunker in case of an attack…maybe built during the Cuban missile crisis." He tempered his enthusiasm long enough to ask, "What do you think?"

"I'm game…let's check the edges for trip wires or security locks." He muttered, "I wonder if these threats have anything to do with our work. I mean…is what we're doing really crapping in someone's backyard?" Stopping, he looked at Chad and said, "You know, you really haven't told me much about what it is we are looking for or what we expect to find down there." With his chin, he pointed at the locker doors in front of them.

Chad shrugged and moved closer to the lockers, pulling out his flashlight to examine the edges. "Doesn't look like anyone has been here recently." He jerked at the two center doors and the opening parted just as he had predicted—two doors on the left and two doors on the right…they were welded together to form one double door on each side. "Well, that part was easy."

Before them was another regular, metal door which opened out and away from them. It had been painted in typical military olive-drab. Stenciled on the door was a warning, 'High powered electrical equipment: Authorized personal only.' At one time the letters had been white, but now they were a dirty yellow—like sour mayonnaise. Several families of insects began scurrying about among the layers of Halloween cobwebs.

"If I had to guess, I'd say this is a dead end." Peterr pulled his flashlight from his back pocket and illuminated the eerie scene. "Well?"

"Guess we better get busy and clear all of this junk out of the way." With a piece of plywood he quickly pushed aside the spider work. "Let's see what the electrical stuff looks like…there's not much likelihood there is any power to this place."

With only a few squeaks, the door opened and revealed a set of concrete steps decending below ground. "What does Sherlock Holmes like to say, 'The game is afoot, Watson.'" Peterr put a tight grip on his flashlight and slowly began down the stairs. The ceiling was rounded and chipped the same way as were the walls. On the ceiling were two sets of what looked like ancient power cables used for lighting. Pieces of plaster had fallen on the steps and made the footing precarious. "I don't see anything that indicates <u>active</u> electricity…yet."

Upon reaching the bottom of the steps, a new hazard lay in front of them. The hallway was about two to three inches deep in what looked like stagnate rainwater. Along the top of the passageway were glass covers for incandescent lights.

"I'm not sure what's down here, but I hope there are no water snakes, or starving rats."

Chad had once been bitten by a snake and was sick for days—every fiber of his body had ached. "Look…I don't think this is going to get us anywhere, it's obvious this is just some old dig done during one of our bouts of national paranoia."

Jokingly, Peterr responded with, "Yeah, like the Civil War." Together they laughed, at least the thought that excursion might end up being a waste of time could be right.

"Ah, crap, we're down here…we might just as well check it out." Chad Buford stepped into the water and winched as the cool, slimy mixture seeped into his shoes. "Come on in, Peterr…the water's fine."

Peterr made a face as he also stepped into the dingy soup. "Okay, but I only have this flashlight…when it goes, I'm out."

"I've got one, but it's a bit smaller…will do in an emergency." Chad moved forward—the water sloshing with every step, and his shadow floating about the walls as Peterr trailed behind him. "Raise your light, Peterr, I think there are some doors just ahead…over on the left side." He dodged his head around until his shadow no longer interfered. "Yeah, that's it."

"Maybe that's the electrical room the sign warned about."

"Let's hope it's not an electrical junction box, Peterr. I don't like standing in water and tinkering with electricity."

"Amen!"

Chad then froze at once and turned toward Peterr and the flashlight, catching his features in one of those poses that creates a grisly face. His eyes widened as he whispered, "Hear that?"

"Hear what?" In a super-hushed voice, Peterr murmured, "Where?"

The sound was unmistakable. At the top of the stairs, the door had just been slammed shut by a deliberate hand which wanted them to know they were now trapped in this oversized catacomb. The reverberation had the effect of making them feel like someone had just dropped the lid on their coffins. They wanted to yell…to tell someone they had just made a mistake, but felt the noise didn't care.

"Oh, crap, Peterr…I think we're in deep stuff now, my boy!"

"Okay…I think it's about time you told me what it is that we're dealing with here, Chad." There was a decided edge to

Peterr's voice and the surroundings began to bring out the emotions of being trapped in a seventieth century basement of a gothic mansion.

Ignoring the emotions of his partner, Chad began considering their options. "Right now we better start thinking of how we are going to get out of this hell hole."

Peterr turned off his flashlight— immediately the tunnel turned into the darkest place that either of them had ever experienced. The sensation was like being trapped alive inside an underwater cave—it even began to feel like the air supply had been cut off. Everything was reduced to one thing, the sound of the water around their feet and the quick, shallow breathing of each man.

"Come on, Chad… Start talking." Even to Peterr the words sounded as if they had appeared out of the darkness. "Jesus, even a cat couldn't see down here."

Chapter 26

Not being home on time was nothing new for Chad Buford, but Sarah had a gnawing tug at the pit of her stomach when he didn't make it home for dinner and didn't call. She tried watching TV but just couldn't get into anything. By seven-thirty, Warren and Glenda were getting on her nerves—she considered putting them to bed but hesitated for fear she might have to leave the house and look for Chad. She knew he was investigating something important but had held off getting into it with him.

Frequently, she got up, pranced about some, then looked out the window to check the street—since her car incident things had been strangely quiet.

She then made a decision. "Kids, put away your things…it's time for bed." Sarah worked hard to keep the edge out of her voice but it still sneaked through.

"Where's Dad? Is he out of town?" Glenda continued picking up her dolls and school books. She had learned when mother was on edge it was not a good time to push. "Is he out of town on business?"

"No…he's at the base. Now put your things away and get to brushing your teeth." She was worried, but even more, she hated she would have to call Marissa to find out if

Peterr and Chad were together. "And make sure your brother picks up his things."

She didn't want to call Marissa while the kids were still up, and it seemed they were taking longer than usual. Glenda had complained it was too early to go to bed— the ensuing argument had not improved her anxieties. When, finally, the children were in their rooms, Sarah stared at her phone like a person examining the best way to squash an intruding insect. Lately, she had developed an aversion to the instrument, but the accusing phone calls had gradually dwindled, although the calls now seemed to be from two different sources. Sometimes, she was not sure the caller really knew with whom they were speaking, as if the words were seriously rehearsed.

With a surge of sudden resolve, she grabbed the phone as if planning to choke the life out of it. The phone rang five times before it was picked up…but no voice answered. "Marissa, it's Sarah…are you there?"

A weak voice responded, "Thank God…it's you!"

In the background Sarah could hear the slosh of ice in a glass. "Are you all right, Marissa?"

"Yeah, just having a glass of iced tea." Another slosh accented her words, "I'm glad you called…I was about to call you. Have you heard from the boys?" She paused, "They were supposed to be back from the base…hours ago." The anger in her voice was only over shadowed by obvious anxiety. "The kids just got back from Hillary's."

Sarah gulped, "I haven't heard from Chad either…they are together, aren't they?"

"Far as I know, yeah." She was slurring her words, and it was obvious the receiver was being moved about. "Bastard, I called him a while ago…he said he would be back in a few hours…I'd turn off the damned phone, but *he* might call."

"Wouldn't he use your cell number?"

"Just as bad. The phone calls are awful…and they won't stop, Sarah…they just won't stop." Marissa faded away to an uncontrollable sob.

"My God!" In disbelief, Sarah realized why Marissa was falling apart. At first, Sarah had thought it might be some kook from the grocery store where she shopped—

after that, she started doing more of her shopping at the base PX. Soon the calls began to take on a more personal tone, implying, but never naming, something from her past. "Is it a man? Does he call only when you are alone?"

"Huh, yeah, how did you know?" Marissa's words were a mix of suspicion and accusation. "You know who it is?" Now her speaking began to take on a harder tone, "If you know who it is…you've got to tell me." She was pleading.

Sarah wished she knew the answer, but just knowing someone else was receiving the same kind of harassment made her feel relieved. "I don't know who it is, Marissa, *but* he, or she, has been calling me too." She paused but Marissa said nothing…all Sarah could hear was hysterical sobbing. "I think it's a man. It could be a disguised voice." At one point, Sarah had thought the calls might even have been coming from Marissa.

"Jesus…I don't know whether to be relieved or more worried. What kind of a person does things like that?" Marissa was sounding as if she were completely sober. "The SOB should be shot! Come to think of it—" She blew her nose and patted at her tear stained eyes, the mascara spread out into a thin black smudge. "I'm not proud of my past, but this…person has no right to harass me like this."

Her words were just as Sarah would have spoken them. She could point out a few blemishes in anyone's life, except there was something mean, accusatory, and cruel about the person who was intruding into their lives. But Sarah was getting fewer calls and now Marissa seemed to be getting more. She paused her thinking and realized at least she wasn't focusing on Chad's tardiness. "Look, Marissa…we're going to have to get together and see what we can figure out."

"Suits me…you free tomorrow?"

"Yeah, just after the kids go to school. Eight thirty work for you?" Sarah was beginning to feel encouraged that, together, they could catch their 'harassers'. Sarah made a mental note to herself to call in some favors and see if she could find out more about Marissa's past…maybe the answers were there.

"Okay, yeah, okay, eight thirty is good. Make lots of coffee." There was a smile in her voice—it was followed by a shuddered sigh of relief. "Oh, and I talked to Peterr late this afternoon. I think I told you that. They were on the base, I think…but he wouldn't give me any details. I was mad at him and, well, I had too much to drink. I only woke up just before you called…when Uncle Blainy brought the kids home. The Colonel said he might check on the guys if we didn't hear from them soon."

It was clear Marissa was getting her "second wind" back. She would talk for hours if Sarah didn't get her off the line, "I'm glad you're better…eight-thirty tomorrow. Hey, Kid, we can fight back…right!"

"Damned right." There was a brief lull and then Marissa said, "You're all right, Sarah…thanks."

"But we first need to locate our men…" Sarah's words fell on a dead phone.

When the phone went blank and the traditional hum commenced, Sarah quickly fell back into her worry about Chad—this was not like him. She was certain something was wrong. Perhaps he had a serious car accident and the police had not yet found him. Again, she tried all of the phone numbers usually answered by Chad. Finally, in desperation, she called his office and requested a trace on his cell.

"Wow! Wherever he is, I can't get a read on him, Mrs. Buford. I can tell he was last located at Field Two. Captain Manning's cell was also there but then they just seem to have disappeared."

Sarah did her best to stay calm, "Can you send a patrol over to that area and check it out…I'm really worried."

"Sure we can, Ma'am. I wouldn't worry too much, Ma'am…you know these GPS systems are good but they're not without their quirks." The operator lowered her voice, "You know…sometimes the boys will shield them so we can't track them to the bars, or some of their other haunts." She giggled like a high-school girl telling her friend a dirty joke.

There was little doubt but what the operator was not taking Sarah seriously. "LOOK! I don't give a damn what problems you have with men in general, but my husband is a Major in the United States military and, by God, you will treat him with some respect." Sarah paused and took a deep breath. "Now get off of your cushy ass and send out a patrol and find out where the Major and the Captain have gone. This could be a serious situation. Understand?"

The response was neither curt, nor rude, but rather a polished military, 'Yesss, Ma'am. We will keep you informed. Is there anything else, Ma'am?'

"No…just get someone out there!" Sarah lowered her voice. "I appreciate it." Only after she got off of the phone did she realize she was shaking. Her fingers were literally vibrating like some alcoholic searching for the last hidden bottle.

*   *   *

A few, small salamanders dashed about the room, the motel at the outskirts of Fort Walton Beach and a favorite place for illegal aliens to gather. The room was dark except for the glow of the mini TV and static hum of a television not long for this world. The man had his arm in a cheap plaster cast, his ribs bandaged with gauze and tape from a local drugstore. The only thing that had brought the two together was, *there would be no statute of limitation for the murder of Charles Buford.*

*   *   *

Chad and Peterr were considering their options, what little they had. In the silence of the underground passageway, all they could hear was the occasional movement by creatures circling in the water and moving about their feet.

In a confidential whisper, Chad said, "Did you hear that?" He leaned close to Peterr's ear, "I think we're not alone…they're closer."

Chapter 27

Leaving a trail of aviation exhaust, the personal jet of Miracle Chu smoothly shot into the early morning sky above Caracas, Venezuela. A rising star known as Earth's sun was making its routine arrival in the east. Patterns of sunlight shifted about the cabin of the Gulf Stream as they adjusted their way through the flight pattern. For a few seconds he could see Ronald's MiG 3 parked off the north end of a remote runway.

Miracle pressed his face against the oval window and looked down toward distant

Lake Maracaibo—without the illumination of the morning light, it looked like a large black diamond which, because of the vast amount of oil produced, was figuratively what it was. He sighed and turned his head to the other side of the cabin and glanced at his lovely 'hostess'—he looked forward to an enjoyable, however brief, trip.

"Excuse me, My Dear, but I must make a rather private call…would you please fix me a cup of tea and take your time about it?" Miracle watched intently as she moved to the galley—approving of her bodily movements but, more than that, he did not want her to overhear the conversation.

After the fourth ring, an electronic voice answered, "Chu Imports…please enter in your personal code." His slim fingers pushed a series of ten digits and then paused—following a tone, he pushed four more buttons. Immediately he heard the sound of four entries being made.

"Chu Imports, how may we serve you?" The voice was both polite and officious.

"Good morning, I would like to place an order for exactly seven baskets of eye glasses." Miracle waited.

"I am sorry, sir, but those only come in fruit jars." A hint of humor trailed the words.

"So, this line is secure?"

"Absolutely, Mister Chu…what is it you would like to discuss?" The tone on the line was still one of a person who was speaking through a voice scrambler.

"I thought I would bring you up to date and check on your progress." The person hearing Miracle's voice was also hearing an electronic version of Miracle's voice.

"Good…I have news for you too."

Chu smiled. "I met with our Venezuelan friend and got things rolling on the money transfers and pieces you requested. Of course our man there is taking care of the books to make sure he is kept in the dark about the government monies."

"Is Hector sold on the project? I am concerned that, now you have left, he will start nosing around…this is a sensitive time. We are so close to completion."

After a brief chuckle, Miracle confided, "I left Ronald there—a thorn in his side you might say. Ronald's presence will keep Hector hopping about…trying to keep track of his pretty ward and Ronald's movements, a distraction…a Trojan horse." He was proud of his many metaphors. "The funds will be in our hands before he has had a chance to realize he is a dead man." Miracle paused for emphasis. "Of course, it will look like the work of a rival drug faction."

The voice responded with an appreciative laugh, "I'd like to see his face when his goon buddies ask him where all the money is." The two voices paused, "Now…I hear we are actually a bit ahead of schedule. We might have to slow things down a bit…but, I don't see it as anything but an operational re-arrangement, not a problem. Right now, our two mice are in the trap—it's just a matter of time."

"I think that will do nicely, My Friend…just remember it is important they be kept alive until we do not need them any longer. Scare them a little, worry their families, mess with their social lives, but we must keep them talking. Do you understand?" Miracle was getting tired, he hated flying and even more he disliked the person with whom he was communicating, but it was necessary if he were to achieve his objectives.

"Most definitely…my people will execute your wishes to the letter. Do not fear."

The old man rubbed his eyes, he could feel a headache coming on, "I never fear…it's a waste of time. I follow the wise words of an American president, 'I trust, but verify, always.'" He pressed a red button and the call ended. *One day I shall have to meet this person who goes by the name of 'Barnacle.'* After reclining his seat, he stretched out and folded his arms across his chest…the drone of the jet engines soon lulled him into a deep sleep.

Barnacle was the code name for what was believed to be a freelance mercenary, as far as anyone knew. Unlike most "for hire" people, Barnacle had become both an assassin and infiltrator with an incredible record of success. Chances were Barnacle did not do, personally, any dirty work…menial tasks farmed out. Speculations were Barnacle was a young man, but others were certain Barnacle was a woman, maybe even an actress who could pass as either. One thing was for sure, whoever Barnacle was—he or she worked like the barnacles on a ship…unseen but always present, always eroding.

However, it was a time for pacing. Barnacle had lied about being ahead of schedule. Perhaps a few things were going well, but the needed scientific data was still being put together. Then there was the matter of an operational test of Susame…it would have to be successful before the partners would invest capital, gobs of it. Now, there was a design problem with rotating the satellite dish. Most of the partners were expecting an energy system while others were bent on a powerful weapon. It couldn't be both. Or could it?

The money to date was just for operating costs, but eventually, Barnacle expected to steal fifty thrillion United States dollars right from under their noses. Barnacle moved to the other side of the room and picked up another secure line, hesitated a moment and gathered his thought before pressing a set a numbers.

"Yes?" The Spanish accent was unusually strong for Hector Rodrigo. This special phone was never used by Hector except when he talked to Barnacle. It had been installed by a person who had never met Barnacle, but followed the instructions as they were given to him. "What is it?"

There was an attitude of irritation in his words.

Barnacle chuckled, "Having trouble with your guest?"

"What? How do you know about my *guest?"* Hector looked around the room as if expecting to see Barnacle hiding behind the draperies or squatted at the back of one of his overstuffed chairs. "That sonofabitch is no gentleman…like a dog in heat he is stalking my little girl."

A sympathetic voice responded, "As a caring father, I am sure you are passionately concerned regarding your rude intruder." An electronic giggle pierced Hector's ear. "I have some good news for you, and an announcement which might upset you." He paused, "But first I want to thank you for your documents on Marissa Manning…very interesting. I assure you I have put it to good use. I also found the papers on the drowning very fascinating. "

Hector sighed and continued looking about the room, not just because of Barnacle but also he ached to know the whereabouts of Victoria and Ronald. "Now what?" Like a person anxious to use the bathroom, he was dancing in place—his eyes rolled about and his head wagged from side to side. "Quit playing and tell me what you want to say…I'm a busy man."

"Did you send my shipment in the manner instructed?" Barnacle had a peculiar way of communicating fear—even over an electronic voice scrambler. "You understand, Hector…your life depends on it."

"Yes, yes, I sent your…*shipment* just as you asked." He used the word *asked* but it was not a request, rather a threat Barnacle would release a wad of information to Hector's business partners if he did not comply.

"And the money, the drugs, they are in route."

Hector paused, "Now, what is it you want to tell me?"

There was a theatrical pause, "I just wanted to encourage you to be especially nice to your guest."

Hector exploded, "That little piece of crap…if it weren't for Miracle, I'd burn the bastard alive just to watch the flesh melt off his bronze body."

"Careful, Hector. Unless I miss my guess, and I never do, your guest is the new head of his father's business."

There was an uncomfortable silence on the line. Hector hesitated to ask, but he could not resist the tease. "Just what are you saying…Miracle just left from my private airport? He is headed for a business meeting." Reluctantly, he admitted, "I don't know where…he didn't say. I think he is headed for Jamaica."

"Yes, I know. By now, he has comfortably drifted into a sleep from which he will not awaken." There was an edge to Barnacle's voice, "You might want to remember that…do not attempt to cross me, Hector. Goodbye—for now."

As the line went into its sing-song humm, Hector could not resist the temptation to look around the room…this Barnacle creep made him shudder, and that infuriated him. What had he tricked Hector into putting on Miracle's Gulfstream Jet? He needed Little One to sooth his nerves. Where was she?

Chapter 28

Chad Buford and Peterr Manning were caged in an underground passageway—reconciling themselves to a desperate situation but when they began to hear movement, goose bumps began to spring up all over their bodies.

Peterr felt an instinct to cry out toward the approaching noises—he wanted to identify his fear. They were standing in water containing, God only knew what, and this was all being done in complete darkness. For all they knew, the noises they now heard could be an immense snake, or a couple of alligators swimming toward the dinner bell.

Sensing Peterr's nervousness, Chad leaned close to the sound of Peterr's heavy breathing. "I think we had better take our chances by trying to find solid ground…quietly, huh?"

Together the two men began pushing their submerged feet through the invisible water which encased their shoes like some alien sludge. Unseen things bumped against their bodies while pieces of loose plaster dropped from the walls and ceiling. But it was the darkness which magnified the fear. Whenever they stopped, Chad and Peterr could hear the swishing of whatever it was following them.

"It's going down." The words whispered out of Peterr's mouth. "Maybe we're…" Peterr bumped his knee against something solid. Quickly he felt at the spot just below his knee—it felt like a cafeteria bench. "I think I just hit a desk or a bench."

Chad swung his arm in the direction of Peterr's voice, "Shshsh…they're gaining on us…I hit something too." He moved closer to Peterr. "Keep moving." Chad could not help but wonder why their trackers had not fired a gun, or turned on a flashlight…all advantages of trackers. Perhaps they even had someone coming at them from the other end of the tunnel. Suddenly, in the distance, he could see a sliver of light—it was too soon to tell if it was natural or electric lights…he hoped it wasn't electrical. "See that?"

"Yeah…what is it?" Peterr began moving his legs even faster; no longer did the noise of their movements preoccupy their thoughts. The lights were moving from side to side rather like the motion of a flashlight. "Oh, my God, they've got us blocked." He felt the surge of adrenalin rip though his body…impulsively, he wanted to hide, but where?

Somebody was calling out. The words were faint and hesitant. Chad grabbed Peterr's arm and waited to hear if the voice called again. There…the voice was more distinct…it was saying something about, 'down hair' no, it was 'down here'.

It was almost like when water is suddenly drained out of one's ear, "Hello…is anyone down here? Major Buford…Captain Manning?"

At first they hesitated and then they heard an explanation, "We tracked your cell phone to this area…are you here?" A pause, then the words continued, "Mrs. Buford told us you were out here. We're police."

Together the men began running though the water, more like the day when they were at the beach. That was where the comparison ended… this place was more like a Parisian sewer—a scene from Les Miserable "We're here…we're here!"

The flashlights moved in their direction, back and forth they swept over the men as if they were lights from a penitentiary tower. Abruptly there was the sound of gun fire. Chad and Peterr dropped into the water…hearts pounding like panicked chickens.

Chad even had time to hear the whiz of bullets miss him only by inches—*they must have hit Peterr*. He wasn't sure…he had been shot before and not felt the pain for some time, but what were they going to do now? They were being chased from behind and shot at from the front…things did not look good. He raised his head out of the putrid water, just enough to see the distant flashlights and listen for another volley of shots. The stench of the odious water caused his eyes to smart. *God…I hope there aren't any pockets of gas.*

So close that Chad was almost on top of him, Peterr could hear his partner moving about in the water. *I wonder if Chad got hit.* The lights were getting closer and the people holding the lights had raised their voices to the point where it sounded as if they were arguing.

Chad turned his head to see how close the pursuers were, sputtering to keep the *sewer water* out of his mouth. Peterr was saying something, but he could not separate the words.

From behind Chad and Peterr, a pistol erupted—sending a flurry of shots so fast it was difficult to count the number of volleys.

"Jesus, Chad, we're trapped."

Without any warning, a puff of fire erupted—quickly, it expanded to fill the entire area of the passageway. The brightness of the flame was intensified against the eerie blackness of the tunnel. A wave of heat began moving, but in the opposite direction of Chad and Peterr. It was moving toward the source…probably a ruptured pipe.

"What the Hell!" Peterr grabbed Chad's arm, "There must be a pocket of methane gas down here."

Between the hail of bullets and the explosion, Chad and Peterr forgot about the flashlights in front of them. The flame was still moving, but at an incredible rate. The question now was, would the flame also move in their direction? Undoubtedly, anyone behind them was probably dead…fried to a crisp.

"Major…Captain… Are you all right?" At the moment, the question was almost absurd. Bullets fired at them and an explosion that shook the concrete walls of a well aged tunnel which could collapse at any moment. "We are Military Police."

Peterr shouted back, "Some police…why did you shoot at us, don't you know who we are?"

A shaky voice responded, "Sir, we were shooting at the three behind you. They had raised weapons and appeared to be an eminent threat."

Apprehension made Chad grab a hold of Peterr. "Wait—" Chad raised his voice, "How did you know they weren't with us?" He glanced back to see if the fire was coming back, but it had apparently blown itself out without coming in their direction.

A different voice responded, it sounded like a young girl, maybe in her late twenties. "Our other team found some guys at the hanger…they put up quite a firefight, two of our men were hit, Sir." The next words had a ring of irritation, "Sirs, we *really* need to get out of here…besides those guys, there…there are a lot of dangerous other things down here."

Peterr and Chad looked toward each other—in the dark it was impossible to tell if they nodded in agreement, but they began to walk toward the flashlights.

The female voice continued, "What were you two doing down here…this old lab hasn't been operational for years."

So it was a laboratory! Chad told himself. In spite of the circumstances, Chad smiled and began to pick up the pace "We must have taken a wrong turn."

The two men chuckled and Peterr added, "You can say that again, Major." He sighed and quipped, "God…I sure could use a hot shower."

A mere twenty feet in front of them, Chad and Peterr reached a series of curved steps much like one would encounter in a lobby. By the time they reached the top step the water was only sole deep. The Air Police hustled them out of the underground swill and into an emerging canapé of nighttime stars. They had been underground a lot longer than they had thought.

"We'd like to see the men you ran into at the hanger…can you take us there now?" Chad ignored the disapproving glance from Peterr Manning.

"Light's not good there, Sir, and the bodies are now at the base morgue. A full investigation of this incident will be underway by 0500, Sir." The female sergeant was one of the shortest and most attractive police officers they had ever seen. Not much more than five foot two; Sergeant Olson's expression was all business…even her blond hair and liquid blue eyes.

"The area, *Sergeant*…we would still like to see the hanger." He had not meant to intimidate her by emphasizing her rank, but it was a habit acquired by his years in the service—especially when he wanted his way. "Please."

Without a break in her expression, Sergeant Olson shook her head, "Right now, Major, I would like to suggest a quick shower. You *gentlemen* smell a lot worse than you think…and you might have some leaches or bacteria that could do harm to your health." She managed a polite grin, "Then we can go to the hanger…I'll have a portable flood light system trucked over to the hanger."

"Thank you, Sergeant, but time is more important than sanitization." Chad moved toward the closest Hum-V. "Coming, Captain?" He could imagine the look on Peterr's face.

The two sojourners tried to slough off their shakes and tremors from the passageway adventure. As casually as possible, they made their way to the vehicle and eased down into the car seats.

Peterr leaned over and muttered, "I think we should have taken those showers first, Major…my butt's wet."

So was Chad's.

Chapter 29

Glistening in the morning sun, water droplets gave off a surrealistic aura about the estate—Victoria's favorite time of day in Caracas, especially looking westward to the high mountains.

Since Ronald Chu had arrived, her days had been filled with a sort of breathless anticipation, no two days ever being the same. While they had never had a sexual encounter, in her young heart she felt as if she were inextricably devoted to him—her true love, her soul mate. Ronald filled her every thought…when he wasn't there, she would soothe her agony with thoughts of her real parents finally finding her and whisking her away from this crass mountain fortress. An unauthorized glimpse into Hector's personal files had given her a brief and somewhat confusing understanding about her past.

A hand lightly touched her shoulder—it was Ronald's and he must have been watching her. "Good morning, Mister Chu."

"Mister Chu is my father, Vicky, remember me…I'm your boyhood friend, the terror of the garden. I used to chase you with earth worms and pet spiders…at least in my pretend memories."

Gently, she tapped Ronald's nose with her index finger. "Yes, and I used to put strange things in your food and hide your favorite set of race cars." She laughed and felt a soft wave of joy—she always felt like this when she was with Ronald. She wished it could always be like this—magically trembling.

Together they walked to the edge of the tile-covered railing and looked down from Hector Rodrigo's beautiful patio. Built to ward off competitors, the previous owner forgot to be concerned about the enemy within his own compound. Hector had either killed or *had* killed his faithful patron and taken everything he possessed. Constantly, Hector worried about the day when the same fate might end his life. Out of his blind fear many a person had been summarily killed…guilty or not.

"Ronald?"

"Yes?"

"Will you ever take me away from this prison?" If someone were watching her, they would have seen a young nineteen year old lady casually moving her head about as she admired the indigenous flora.

This was not the first time she had asked this very question, but it was the first time he could seriously consider her plea. "You know my father is missing, Victoria. Right now, it is important I return to China and protect the family interests." He turned and faced her, "I cannot afford to antagonize Hector…at least not at this time. We are working on an important deal and need him." He paused and looked around, "If my father is dead, and I think he might be, I must take over the operation of our family business…but it will also give me the power to take you away from here. No one would dare to challenge me, Vicky, no one…not even Hector. In fact, if I find out he had anything to do with my father's assumed demise, well…"

She blinked as the tears began to slide from her lower eye lids. "If I know Hector…he will consider it a chance to win your friendship. He's such a bastard, Ronald." For the first time that morning she looked into his eyes and searched his soul. *He really loves me…I know he does.* "You know I love you, Ronald…not just as a woman, but as something more deep. I don't know the words, but I know I want to grow old with you. I want to make your every day the happiest any man has ever experienced." She glanced toward the office area where she knew Hector would be watching—her lips pushed together and she sighed in pain. "I just want to hold you until the day God takes us both to heaven."

Ronald, too, looked at the building, "Vicky…it hurts my heart every day you suffer here." He reached out with his hands and gently held her cold fingers. "I will make it all up to you…soon. In the meantime, you must stay safe."

He dropped his head, "Something has come up in Florida…rather unexpected." Effortlessly he moved her hands to his lips and kissed the back of her hand. "I will also use the time to search out my father… I only pray he is still alive. I have much I should have said to him."

She moved close to him and looked up, "Hector is not to be trusted, Ronald. I know you know that, but I don't think you realize how insane he can be."

Ronald moved her hand to her side—the side away from the view of the building. "Here, I want you to have this…it's small, but in the right place it will do the job."

In the palm of her hand she could feel the weight of the small pistol, feeling strangely cold—like death itself. She would like to speak, but the vision of actually shooting someone, even the loathsome Hector, was suddenly a feasible reality. "I…don't know…if I could…do it, Ronald."

"Let's hope you don't have to, but there is no telling how he will react to my visit, or if my father is still alive." He smiled at her, "Keep it someplace safe—it's something new, experimental. It's electronic…absolutely silent."

Victoria and Ronald turned their heads toward the building—a door had just slammed shut. Hector Rodrigo was headed their way. In each of his hands he held a glass of what looked like orange juice.

"Ah, I see you two are enjoying the view," Hector said. "Magnificent is it not? Don't get too close to that edge…it's a long way down." To each of them he handed a glass. "Fresh squeezed…I have them grown just for us." It was obvious he was hiding his seething jealousy. He turned to face Ronald, "I have been burning up the communication lines, but it seems no one has any news about your father, My Boy…sorry."

Ronald was well aware of the insult intended by the expression, "My Boy," it was meant to demean him in the eyes of Victoria and remind him of his lack of experience in the world of criminals. "He's alive, Hector…I can feel it." Without drinking the juice, Ronald bent down and set it on the ledge of the wall. "I will find him, and we will discover the cause of his sudden disappearance. Right now, I have our men working on a satellite search and tracking the movements of his plane."

"There is no doubt, but what Miracle would be very proud of your loyalty…the mark of a true son, would you not say so, Victoria." As he spoke, Hector had snapped his head in her direction as if to catch her in mid thought. She had not jumped the way she usually displayed her fear. "Victoria?"

Her mind was whirling…she felt the power of the pistol in her hand. Like a living creature it was throbbing in her hand…she could feel its pulse, its life's purpose. As if Hector had suddenly turned into a harmless puppy, she looked at him…the man she had grown to hate and fear, the man who had humiliated her and ruined her childhood. The pistol had a life of its own. "Hector?" "Yes, My Dear?"

Victoria moved close to him. She rose up on her toes and placed her mouth close to his cheek. Out of the corner of her eye she watched his smirk of satisfaction. The jolt of the bullet that moved through his vital organs took a few moments before he could react. He tried to jump back, because of the soft noise, but could only look down at the blackish red fluid pumping out of his chest.

Strangely, it had not sounded like a pistol shot—she looked at the snub nosed barrel and realized it had nothing on the end. It was the latest thing in weaponry…it barely made a sound, like the air blowback of a bee-bee gun. Electronic operated, not gas operated. Even though the shot had been quiet, birds scattered from the nearby trees—they screamed their alarms and broke the morning silence with the beating of their wings.

So swiftly did Ronald grab the weapon from her hand, she could feel a blood blister forming on her finger. He wiped the weapon clean and returned it to the inside of his jacket. It was a forensic nightmare—no prints, no gun residue and no barrel trace. Next he looked at the entrance to the wound. Besides being the latest thing in silencers, the device also eliminated the markings of signature residue from close shots. The blood made it difficult to tell, but it looked like no one would be able to tell he had been shot at close range. Ronald yelled, "Help…help…Hector has been shot!"

Hector's eyes were moving, but slowly glossing over. It was doubtful he even knew what happened. Blood was beginning to drift into the cracks and crevices of the tile. Like all liquid, the blood was objectively seeking the lowest level. His mouth was moving much like a fish gasping for oxygen. Ronald had seen men die and so had Victoria. She had seen so many of the helpless people depart the world as Hector had butchered just because he felt insecure or was insulted by them. She wondered how he would have enjoyed seeing his own demise, as amusing as all the others?

There was no love lost between Hector and his bodyguards or, for that matter, his household staff—where most were forced to work for him. Hector had a nasty habit of recruiting his workforce by threatening to torture or kill those whom they loved, and therefore, his death would not be any great loss to them. In the end, it was a peculiar way to buy loyalty.

Quickly, Ronald explained how Hector had been facing the wall while He and Victoria were looking in the other direction. Ronald recounted how a lone gunman had fired a shot from the other side of the wall…Victoria and he had dropped to the ground and the gunman had disappeared before they could get a look at him. The speculation was the killer had escaped by parachute or by spelunking.

Ronald took Victoria aside, "You had better leave with me…get your things, but only what you must have."

She nodded and bolted for the mansion. One of the first things on her list was

Hector's entire file on her birth and adoption, which she had already saved via flash stick.

Chapter 30

My God, Chad! What in the hell were you doing mucking about in that ancient sewer?" Sarah said, hands on hips. Her eyes were discharging fire at her husband. At one point she thought he had been killed or died from some accident. "Well? I'm waiting"
In spite of himself, Chad burst into a broad smirk—a genuine Cheshire cat grin. She should have seen him *before* he was cleaned up. Later, he would have to tell her about the bully sergeant who shoved Peterr and him into the 'drunk tank' showers at the AP station. "Honey, we were just checking out some leads in a case we're working…I guess we must have stepped on some toes." He tried to grab her into a hug, but she was having no part of it.
Heads moved from side to side as Warren and Glenda watched their parents spar over the events of the night before. Eagerly, they anticipated the time when the arguing would

end and their father would tell them all the exciting events of his latest adventure. To the children, it was not as if their indestructible father was ever in any real danger, it was more like listening to the events of their favorite superhero.

Sarah tried to give the narration her full attention but images of the skating pond flashed significantly.Twenty years ago she had decided to put the incident out of her mind, but, now, here it was again—sharper and clearer than ever. It was a fact…she was responsible for the death of Chad's brother, Charles. How could she ever tell him?

* * *

"It wasn't as bad as you think, Marissa. Sure there were some bad guys following us, but it all turned alright." Peterr Manning opened the door of his white, twenty-five cubic foot refrigerator and snatched out a bottle of A&W Root Beer. "I'm surprised you were sober long enough to know I was missing." Before the words left his mouth, he regretted his outburst. His whole face tightened until resembling a plump raisin.

She snarled and glared at him. "You sonofabitch, don't you EVER talk to me like that. Do you even have any idea how much I have given up just because I married a second rate jar-head?" With a hand that was shaking with rage, Marissa dumped another round of shots into her half-full glass. "I had it made. I was the bell of the ball. When I had my "coming out" I could have married any one of a dozen rich kids, but no… I had to get bedded by the likes of you." She banged her glass on the bartop and began to cry.

Peterr had seen this act before…one minute she could seem cold sober and the next, she was falling down drunk. The story was always the same…he had ruined her perfect life. This is where she usually inserted a blip about her dead cousin, Heather. There was a real irony to her self-pity—he knew she loved him and adored Carl and Betsy, but since she had been getting the mysterious phone calls she had turned into an insufferable witch. Unfortunately, she would not discuss what was going on…she insisted they were just prank calls, but he did not believe her.

"Mar, I know you're upset. I'm sorry I made you worry so much. You know the kind of job I have…sometimes there are risks—I deal with criminals." He moved closer to her and put an arm around her shoulder—she leaned her head against him. He was surprised—her breath did not reek of alcohol—he thought she had been drinking scotch. "You should lie down and get some rest… Here, I'll take your drink."

"Like hell you will." She jerked back her glass, but in doing so, she spilled the entire contents. "I'm going to bed…alone." She turned and began walking down the hallway—she raised her hand and said, "Better say good night to the kids."

"Sure." When he heard her door close, Peterr picked up her empty glass, cautiously giving it a sniff… *Scotch…but weak,* he told himself. He held the glass at a distance as if checking to see if he actually had the right glass. Tenderly, he set the glass down and began drumming his fingers next to the questionable object. *Maybe that is why she put it down. If not, what was she up to…since when did she drink weak, watered down booze?*

"Daaad?" The chiding voice of his daughter whispered to him. "You promised." Now her tone was flooded with intended guilt.

Peterr turned toward Betsy and gave her his most fatherly smile. "Be right there, Pumpkin." He actually wanted to put his questioning mind to rest. Too much had happened over the last twenty-four hours for him to continue at his present pace. Sagging his shoulders, he made a display of being beaten by his precious daughter. "You win, My Queen…your slave is at your command.""Oh, Daddy, you're so silly." Betsy giggled and was happy again.

He loved to hear her giggle, just to clean the air. Her simple joy always seemed to put life in perspective. Peterrr picked up speed and began dashing for her room. "I'll show you who's silly." It would be tickly time for Betsy and Carl—questions about Marissa would have to wait.

Marissa often wondered how her life would have been much different if Charles Buford had not been killed at the pond—

Chapter 31

The plane would have normally gone directly northwest, but impressed by the view of Lake Maracaibo, Miracle had instructed the pilot to go west before going north to Santiago de Cuba—he had even considered a brief stop at Barranquilla, Columbia. It was one of those serendipitous acts of life that escapes the logical mind, but often saves a life…and so it did for Miracle Chu. His Gulf Stream jet made a "forced landing" just past the fifty-eight hundred foot mountain, Pico Cristobal Colon. The pilot, co-pilot and the attendant were all killed on impact. Alone, cold, and as angry as he had ever been in his life, Miracle was about eighty miles east of Soledad, Columbia, at an elevation of about one thousand feet—it was wet and showed no signs of drying out.

As he could best tell, the cabin climate control system had begun omitting some sort of gas that put everyone to sleep. If they had gone directly northwest, as intended, they would have crashed into the Caribbean Sea and been written off as another Bermuda Triangle phenomenon. Now that the aviation fuel had dissipated, he was able to hunker down in the cabin and wrap himself in blankets.

"Ronald will find me, Ronald will find me, Ronald will find me—" Over and over he repeated the words—words of faith in his son. For now, his belief his son loved him, would search for him, was the only thing keeping him alive. For one of the few times in his life, Miracle felt old…like when his wife died.

As the second night of loneliness would soon be approaching, he fought against the same feelings. Several hundred feet away, in a broken section of the aircraft, was a battery operated signal…a distress call that automatically emitted the GPS location of the downed aircraft. The battery was damaged and would probably only operate for a few more hours at best. More to the point, who would think to look so far off course?

Chapter 32

Barnacle was furious. The Susame Project was falling apart—Miracle Chu was missing but now Hector Rodrigo would have to be dealt with…and the Florida team had gone too far with their incompetence and was now compromised. The brief trip to Cuba had not been Barnacle's idea, but Miracle had insisted on a rendezvous in order to sort out the funds collected by the interested parties. Barnacle was certain there was no way to avoid the truth, but he had another agenda --one meant to benefit himself. Fifteen nations had begun to bid on a share of the profits from blackmailing the world with the doomsday weapon. It was a good start.

Not that Barnacle would have actually met with Miracle—Barnacle's identity was something religiously guarded. If Miracle had not insisted on the meeting, Barnacle would not have found it necessary to have Hector participate in the crash of Miracle's aircraft, but Barnacle could feel the tentacles of the old Chinaman reaching out, even now…they were getting too close for comfort. With the old man out of the way, Barnacle would encourage Hector to eliminate Miracle's young son—a task he was sure Hector would enjoy, however Barnacle had not yet recived the new about the demise of his South American collaborator.

No doubt, the money would have to be moved…Hector was never to be trusted anyway, but there was a good possibility Miracle had said something to his son,

Ronald. Barnacle made a face—Hector had not checked in for two mornings. At best, Hector was not a man to be trusted, but where money was concerned he was usually prompt. Today, Barnacle expected a large shipment of drugs to be smuggled into the port of Miami, Florida. With a disgusted shake of the head, Barnacle concluded Hector was probably indulging himself with one of his many senoritas.

Barnacle had bigger concerns than dealing with a demented South American Want-ta-be. In a matter of days the first scheduled test of Susame would take place…most everything was ready to go but, if everything was to come off as planned, timing was crucial. For one of the few times Barnacle could recall, beads of nervous sweat began to appear. The real secret concerning Susame was going to come out some day, but if it were revealed too soon, Barnacle would be ruined or, more likely, dead.

What is keeping that idiot? Barnacle wanted to get a report on the crashing of Miracle's airplane. With a nervous hand, Barnacle reached for the secured-line phone and placed a call to the home of Hector Rodrigo in Caracas, Venezuela. The phone pulsed as it usually did, but no accented voice answered. "Something is wrong? I can feel it in my gut." Quickly, Barnacle put down the phone and placed another call to Caracas.

"Olla, I mean, 'Hello'…I was expecting your call." The female voice was solicitous and hushed.

"I have not heard from my mountain friend…what is happening?" Barnacle's electronic voice cracked in an eerie mechanical tone.

The voice in Caracas became even more hushed. "He is dead…"

"What…what happened?" Barnacle's words were clinical.

"They say someone shot him…he is most dead, really."

Sharply, he said, "Who?"

"We don't know. Mister Miracle's son and Victoria were on the back patio. We think someone shot at Mister Ronald, but killed Mister Hector…dead."

I didn't order anything like that. Barnacle was silent while the report was considered. "Are they still there?"

"Who?"

"Ronald and Victoria— who would you think I would mean?" There was a definite edge to Barnacle's voice. "Are they still there?"

"Oh, yes, but I think they are leaving for the airport, Mister Ronald has his plane there." The woman was anxious to terminate the conversation with Barnacle. "I did nothing wrong…I just give you the story…no?"

Barnacle hesitated, "What about Miracle?"

The voice brightened, "We did just as you said…his plane is gone. We hear nothing from him." There was a self-satisfied smile in her voice, "We did a good job, no?"

With a deep sigh, Barnacle put down the phone and began to think. *Killed…Hector killed? I didn't order anything like that. I wasn't finished with him, yet. So who else would want him dead? The list is too long to narrow down now.*

Barnacle began to laugh, "The kids did it! I'll bet the kids killed that Spic reprobate." In spite of Barnacle's irritation concerning the death of an underling, Barnacle began to shout. "Good for them! It couldn't have happened to a more deserving pervert!"

But, gradually, Barnacle began to realize the impact on the Susame Project. "Damn it!!!" Barnacle's plans went far beyond dollars and cents—ambition and power were the objective…the money was just a means to get there.

Chapter 33

On of the last things Hector did was to bribe the right officers, he had managed to get permission for Ronald to relocate his private plane at a remote military airfield. As Ronald and Victoria arrived, there was a crowd of discrete onlookers checking out his plane—undoubtedly a first look at a Russian MiG-31BM.

To a casual observer, the high speed multifunctional long-range jet fighter would appear to resemble an F-14 Tomcat or the F-15 Eagle. By an agreement with the Russian government, the Chinese first bought 24 MiG-31 Foxhound long-range interceptors in 1992. Miracle had been financially involved in the set-up factory at Shenyang so when the upgraded BM model was produced in 1999 he "negotiated" a deal to present one to his son, Ronald. The gift was a sort of graduation trophy for completing his fighter training—three of the best combat pilots Miracle could hire devoted eighteen months to the boy's training. Ronald turned out to be what the trainers called a "natural combat pilot."

As they arrived at the airfield, Victoria looked out the window of the car to study the aircraft design; the seventy foot length and forty-five foot wing span a jaw–dropping sight. "This is your plane?"

Proudly, Ronald replied, "Yeah, she's big and fast—does mach two point eight three…and that's world class." He tipped his head and grinned at her. "I had a little trouble finding a flight suit for you, but I think it will fit okay."

"We're flying in THAT?" She didn't know if she was thrilled or scared out of her mind.

"Think of it as the latest Walt Disney ride in Anaheim…you'll love it."

Except for her trust in Ronald and their need to get out of reach of Hector's "friends," she would not have even considered sitting in the awesome looking fighter. She gulped, "Okay…if you say so. What do I do? What's a 'fashionable' suit?"

Ronald could not help himself--he laughed. "Hey, don't worry…I've got a job for you to do…and the word is 'flight suit'—not fashionable, but you'll need it. It'll be just like watching a video game."

As they approached the aircraft, an armed guard challenged them…Ronald was pleased to see they had been guarding his beauty just as they had promised.

Closer to the MiG-31BM, Ronald changed his tone and asked her, "Do you know why they call these fighters, 'MIGS'?"

"I thought it was just because it was a cool name."

He shook his head, "Most people think that, but it was named after Mikoyan and Gurevich, two Russian guys who teamed up to produce this series of aircraft. Pretty neat, huh? Having a famous plane named after yourself?" Pointing at a man who was running on a course to intersect with their car and his MiG, Ronald muttered, "There's the guy who has your flight suit, Victoria…like I said, it's not fashionable, but you'll need it."

After forty-five minutes of preparations, Ronald and Victoria bolted down the runway, the jet engines at full power and the front wheel gently lifting off the ground. He always liked this part—when all the heads turned to watch as his plane sliced into the heavens. It made him feel as if he possessed all the power of the plane. It was God-like.

"You okay?" Ronald's voice filled Victoria's head. She had been so intent on the view and the ride she literally jumped in her seat.

"WOW! This is great, Ronald…your Dad bought you this?"

Ronald was busy talking with the flight-control operators and making a controlled turn towards the west; "Yeah…a little more expensive than a Rolls, huh?" That remark was a quote from one of Miracle's favorite retorts. "Watch the screen in front of you."

Victoria jerked back as the screen illuminated with a picture which looked familiar to her. "Is this the way past the lake?"

"Yeah…Maracaibo, and then over toward Barranquilla. Dad filed a flight plan to go directly to Cuba, but he told me he was going West and then North…just for security reasons."

"So…what are you looking for, Ronald?'
She squirmed about in the tight confinement
of her seat.

"That's your job back there. Look for a
blip on the screen; it will look like a stick-
figure person, only red." He cut her off as
he again talked to the ground towers, and
then he adjusted his flight path…for his
fighter; he was traveling as slowly as he
could. "I'm covering the ground faster than
I would like, but we should be able to get a
good read on Dad."

"You mean the plane?"

"No, but, well, yeah…the plane *and* my
Dad—he has an implanted chip. The chip
will even tell us what his medical condition
is…if he crashed or landed somewhere
along this path."

"You said a *red* stick figure?
"Yeah, you bet. I see it too, Vicky." In
Ronald's mind he could see Miracle waving
to him as the stick figure appeared. He
spoke to the onboard computer, "Display."
A multicolored screen lighted and began
displaying the medical condition of
Miracle…dehydrated, fatigued, but all of the
vital signs were still green. "There he
is…see that figure on the screen? Looks like

he's okay, Victoria. Now, we need to get him out of there." Ronald tried to remain calm as he thought threw the options.

"Did anyone else survive?" Her stomach lurched as he banked his plane to the right.

"Could be, but I don't know. The Gulfstream's transponder is still sending out a signal, but it's getting weak. The trees might have cushioned the crash." Right now, Ronald wished he had a helicopter, as the jet was too fast to really look at anything.

"How are you going to get them out of there? You know, that's pretty dense jungle." For a brief moment, Victoria had a flash of the time Hector had taken her on one of his hunting trips—she shuddered at the thought.

Ronald didn't answer, but instead was on his headset talking to someone he knew in the Columbia drug trade. There was little doubt he could get someone to rescue his father, but then, they would probably inform the wrong people. For now, it was best they thought Miracle was dead…or at least missing. In order to make this "hush-hush" retrieval happen, he could not use a

helicopter…it would have to be an overland
job.

When Ronald stopped talking, Victoria
asked, "Who were you talking to? Someone
in Caracas?" She was felling nervous.
What if Ronald were not the person she
thought he was—it had happened to her
before. "Are they after us?"

He ignored her paranoia, "I don't really
know the guy…he's an old friend of my
father's. They served together in the army
but he now runs a sizeable drug trade in this
area. My father was thinking of dropping in
on him anyway, that's why he took this
detour in his trip to Cuba." Ronald banked
left and sighed, "I only hope he is as
trustworthy as Dad thinks he is."

Victoria barely listened—her heart was
beating with fear as she considered how
Hector would have treated her if he had
survived the shooting. She had seen how he
would torture victims for days before
granting a slow and painful death. "Oh!"

"We can't land at any of the airfields here.
It's too risky…I probably wouldn't get my
plane back." He felt a sense of relief now
that he had arranged for his father's
rescue…but he still had a nagging fear as he

delivered him into the hands of someone that Ronald did not know. "We could land in Cuba, but I think we had better fly on to Florida." He hesitated, as he pursed his lips and considered. "There is someone I think you ought to meet."

She shrugged, "And just who would that be, Ronald?"

"A friend of your mother, Vicky." He could hear her gasps as he paused, "that is…if you would like to."

An old saying shot through her mind. *Be careful what you wish for…you might get it.*

Chapter 34

There was no doubt the events of the past week were the talk of the Air Force base. By now the underground tunnels on the base were being explored by authorized personnel from a number of different departments…even civilians with pass privileges came on base to experience the adventure of exploring the "secret" caves. Chad Buford and Peterr Manning had been grilled until their ears burned and hind quarters felt like a trucker's worn out seat cushion.

Chad rubbed his face with his dry palms. With his fingertips he massaged his tired eyes. "Honestly, Peterr, I'm sorry I dragged you into this mess." He held up his hand when Peterr began to speak. "I know you volunteered, but you really didn't know what you were getting into."

He would have to admit he had enjoyed the distraction—ever since he had discovered Marissa might not be the drunk she appeared to be. Peterr Manning had been racking his brain to piece together a considerable number of events from the past. Had she been inebriated, or not…was she just faking now, or was this an isolated incident? There was no way he could question her without tipping her off he knew she had been cutting her drinks. Maybe she had been using water for gin or vodka…the possibilities drove him nuts. "I told you before, Chad, think nothing of it. It was great…a little scary at times, but great. I wouldn't have missed it for the world." He leaned forward and shook his head, "I still don't fully understand this Susame thing you mentioned, but it must be important."

After a wry grin and a muffled snicker, Chad sniffled and tipped his head toward the ceiling. "You might say that…it's supposed to be the New World's doomsday blackmail threat…then, again, it could be the device which will provide cheap energy and climate control to all the peoples of the world. Take your pick. You know, just the latest in an attempt to hold the world hostage while a bunch of criminals take control of the world's governments and religions."

"I've heard that song before, but there is no way they could actually use the thing as a weapon without killing themselves." An interesting question but one that, at the moment, didn't have an answer.

"That's probably true, Peterr, and I think they would hesitate, but on the other hand these kinds of people would rather be dead than give up their power." Chad wagged his head and lamented, "Faced with that alternative I think they would blow the whole planet apart…eons ahead of schedule." He leaned forward only a few inches from Peterr's nose. Chad could feel the other man tense up. "Don't worry, Peterr, I'm not going to kiss you." Chad smiled, "The problem with this thing is …it, supposedly, can be controlled to where it can take out a single bug—yeah, that

small…or it can take out our entire planet."
Chad felt a cold chill slither up his spine,
"There are even some religious people who
want the world destroyed because they
believe it will usher in the arrival of their
spiritual leader.

"Oh, my God…can it really do that?" It
was a rhetorical question. "With a weapon
that versatile, how can they control it? Who
has it? Is it already in use? Peterr Manning
was chattering like a three-year-old asking
"Why, Why, Why?" "I'm sorry, Chad, but
who has this thing and how long have you
known about it?"

Chad pulled back. "Easy, Peterr…the
answer to most of your questions is, "I don't
know," at least not yet. Rumor has it they
plan to stage a test of the Susame beam, and
perhaps within the week. Sometime soon,
they will start bidding for the rights to
control the thing. You can't keep something
like this a secret, though they try. Word gets
out one way or the other. I couldn't tell you
if that will be the energy machine, or the
weapon…or both." In a gesture of
frustration, he threw his hands into the air.
"You see…it is the same device, just a
question of how they use it. The thing will

always be a threat, even if used for cancer research."

"So what were we looking for in those tunnels under the base?" Peterr was biting his lower lip…he could hardly believe what he was hearing—all of his worries about Marissa were fading away; at least they weren't churning his gut."Hey, wasn't there a story about a genious scientist who was supposed to have built a 'doomsday' ray?'

"I heard that 'urban legend' too, but I don't know anyone who could prove it was built or actually would work. To tell the truth…I really got nothing…at this point." Chad walked toward the window and motioned for Peterr to follow him. When he got close he said, "Everything in this house could possibly be bugged…okay?"

"Sure…got cha." He looked around as if expecting to see devices or people peeking out of corners or behind mirrors.

"We haven't had much luck. Not one bread crumb to follow…at least nothing which really gave us the results we wanted or expected." He paused, "Sarah and I, well, mainly I, met a group of scientists who gave me some information about the project, but they were too cryptic to provide any insight." He shrugged, "So I pulled a bluff and tried to ruffle a few feathers…you and I got some response the other night. I don't think they really wanted to kill us. It was more like a move to…discourage us."

"Okay, you've got my attention. So…what do we do now?"

"Let's go outside for a bit." The two men walked through the backyard and leaned against a fence about fifty feet from the house.

"Safe place?" Peterr began a discreet scan of the surroundings.

"I don't know, probably." Chad turned his face toward the fence. "What I'm about to tell you must not reach another person's ears. No one, period—"

Peterr nodded.

"I just got a message from a contact I trust. We are about to be visited by the son of a very powerful Chinese industrialist by the name of Miracle Chu. Heard of him?"

"Only the name, but his son, Roger, I believe…is just some sort of playboy isn't he?"

"His name is Ronald and, yes, he seems to get around, but I wouldn't believe everything we hear or read. He has an

American education and is expected to take over when his father dies." Chad paused, "Incidentally, there is a rumor that his father is…missing."

"Assassinated?"

"No…well, maybe. I'm not certain, but Chu's private jet never made it to Cuba. It is presumed down somewhere in the Caribbean." Chad Buford took a deep breath as if to calm himself down. "My informant only had time to give me a sketch about what has been going on in South America."

Looking totally confused, Peterr wrinkled his face, "What in the world would a Chinese businessman and a South American have in common?"

"There are lots of Asians in South America, Peterr…and not all of them are Communists. I have been able to find out some Chinese and some South American drug lords are partners in this project. So far, I think they have kept the Arabs out of the loop." Chad looked at Peterr and shrugged, "Oh, yeah, the Venezuelan drug lord, Hector Rodrigo, has been wounded…maybe killed."

"Jesus, Chad, how do you know all of this? Who's your informant?" He knew he wasn't going to get an answer, but the words just slipped out of his mouth.

"Ahhh…not so fast, Buddy." He smiled, "You know the line, 'If I told you…I'd have to kill you.'" Chad Buford had considered telling Peterr Manning about the existence of a mysterious personage some called "Barnacle," but decided against it.

Chapter 35

Just west of Panama City, Florida, outside the low tide maritime limits, a three hundred foot vessel rested at anchor, its exterior painted as if primed for a complete repaint job; patches of black, gray, white, speckled every inch of the formidable looking freighter—the look also serving as a practical but inconspicuous camouflage. A layer of large metal containers were lashed to the deck—usually filled with automobiles on their way to dealers in the United States—but not today.

Upon close examination, one would discover only a few of the containers were occupied with vehicles—most of them fitted together to form a large area devoted to laboratory work and testing areas. Access to the holds below was made through a series of elevators and stairs hidden from outside view. An outer hull on the containers allowed them to be dropped over the side and sink to a floating depth of fifty feet without seriously damaging the inner contents.

In bright white letters the stern of the vessel bore the registry of the nation of Malaysia. The registration papers indicated she was a ship owned by the Malaysian government and not any private company or individual. One might say, "The ship had diplomatic immunity."

Below deck, the scientific teams were preparing to activate an orbiting satellite positioned so it was always in line with the fiery star called The Sun. Purposely; the satellite design was similar in appearance to the SOHO satellite which is used to study the magnetic loops of the sun.

The satellite was perched in one of the gravity balance spots called an "L" zone (Lagrange Point). First the beams would fire and destabilize the magnetic belt of the sun. The sun would respond by producing solar flares. The satellite would then destabilize a spot in the earth's magnetic belt and allow the solar flare to strike the earth with its full force. The effect would be cataclysmic.

In less than forty-eight hours the Susame Beam was scheduled to be released toward the military post designated as Eglin Air Force Base—positioned on the outskirts of Fort Walton Beach, Florida. The base had been chosen as the announced target because of its position on a peninsula and because of its scientific and military strength. Both militarialy and politically the strick would prove the point the cartel was open for a thriving blackmail business.

At the appointed time, the ship would be evacuated and the surviving crew, along with those valuable to the project, would be evacuated to Cuba. There, they would be able to observe the fruits of their labor.

The clock was ticking, when a low flying Mig31BM passed overhead on its way to landing at Eglin.

* * *

Ronald had just completed a follow-up conversation with his contact in Columbia and knew he had to stay on top of it all or his Dad ran the risk of not seeing another sunrise. "Looks like they are on their way to rescue Dad…I don't know how he survived that crash. Maybe that's why they keep calling him "Miracle.""

Victoria painted on a tense smile which she knew Ronald Chu could not see, "Any news about Hector, or what's happening in Venezuela?"

The ship below Ronald did not distract him even for one second—it was a freighter ship just like thousands of others he had seen. He replied to Victoria, "Nothing new…I've got to talk to the military control tower, Vicky. These guys are really sticklers with this air space…I'll talk to you later." He clicked off and then back on, "Enjoy the view." Ronald held back the information Hector's security team was combing the hillside for signs of the assassin, but not with a lot of enthusiasm.

Every time the jet hit an air pocket, Victoria Rodrigo would gulp and clutch her sensitive stomach. The view was spectacular—below her, she could see the incredible shades of green and blue of the Gulf of Mexico, and just ahead the vast expanse of the Caribbean Sea and the wide-reaching Atlantic Ocean. Ronald had slowed to approach speeds, the canapé below resembling the artistic canvas of a Claude Monet painting. She was still confused and restless about Ronald's question, "meet a friend of her mother," and why had they not discussed the reason Miracle's private plane crashed? So many unanswered questions, but they would all have to wait. She took a deep breath as Ronald went to full flaps and tweaked his after-burners.

Chapter 36

If things went as planned, the slippery Barnacle would forever vanish. This plan had been ten years in the making and finally at hand—it was also true that Barnacle's plans contained another option. If the plan failed, instead of a life of ruling and controlling things and people, Barnacle had decided it would be time to cash in all the chips and disappear, but only *if* things did not go as planned.

A concealed receiver vibrated on Barnacle's leg. "Yes?"

"They are landing at Eglin…just thought you would want to know." There was a pause, but Barnacle said nothing "Is there anything you would like to have happen to either of them?"

"Miracle's son may prove a problem…kill him, but do not touch the girl. She could prove useful." The electronic voice scrambler crackled, "Do you understand me?"

"Of course…I'll take care of it personally." His voice showed how nervous the man was.

"The Rodrigo job was a real mess. Did you have anything to do with that?"

Confused, the voice grew edgy, "I thought you had arranged that little thing. I didn't have anything to do with it." Pause, "You know it was Hector who had the Chink's plane tampered with."

"Yes…I know, and I also know Miracle most probably survived the crash. I'm not sure of the information sold to me, but I will let you know if it needs some fixing." Barnacle laughed, "That stupid Hector never could do anything right. For all the years I have known him he has just continued to disgust me. That should be…he *used* to disgust me."

A change of subject seemed to be in order, so the caller said, "We are ready for the test…are you anticipating any changes? Should any of our people leave the test area?"

It was a catch question—the actual objective was to remain unknown to anyone but Barnacle. Each potential target was only identified by a set of numbers and Barnacle would provide the final test set of digits. "That is not my prerogative…I will let you know when the decision is made." It was Barnacle's policy to always indicate Barnacle was simply a highly-placed employee…so far, it had afforded a great line of protection. "I must go now…I will call you when I need you."

There was a hidden fact Barnacle did not want anyone to know. Only Barnacle knew the truth and it was not going to be revealed before its time. According to their studies, the Susame Beam could activate a volcano, open a fault line, destroy a town, or just turn an individual person into a pile of cinder ash. It was a powerful weapon…the kind rulers and armies had pursued for centuries. The peculiar thing was, as an energy producer, it was almost as dangerous to the holder as it would be as a weapon. *If* a product like this could be produced…with whom should it be entrusted? In fact, not even Barnacle would be safe…a fact Barnacle had known for some time; however, the money which could be extorted was fantastic.

Barnacle struggled with the dilemma—it would have to be addressed at a later time. Right now it was time to go to the air force base and greet the new arrivals, with all the gockers there, he was certain he would not be noticed. "It should be interesting." Ronald had served a purpose and now it would be time to dispatch him before he ruined things.

A door opened behind Barnacle, the smell of afternoon rain was in the air. Children were playing hopscotch, and a small dog was barking in hopes of participating in the games. It was just a typical day in the neighborhood. Barnacle spoke to the man, "I'll be at Base Three—"

The man raised his hand in a snappy salute, "Will do."

Without ceremony, Barnacle threw a cap into the back seat and slipped behind the wheel of the four door sedan. Barnacle hated this time of the day when everything was so quiet—reflecting on the events in the life of a super-spy was not Barnacle's most favorite thing. *By God, when this thing is over I am going to disappear and finish out this life in peace.* He often spoke in this way, but it did not fit in with his real goal. Barnacle knew it was more likely a quiet death was waiting but, for now, that thought would have to be put aside. With the car in drive he pressed on the accelerator and headed for the air field…there were people to be met…duties to be performed, tests to be accomplished.

Chapter 37

Looking more like the arrival of a foreign dignitary than the landing of two young people fleeing South America, the MiG settled gently on the tarmac. The markings on the aircraft seemed odd—it was a very sophisticated fighter jet, the kind which usually has the logo of some rival nation, but this one had the words, "Chu Exporters." The MiG gave a roar like a challenging lion on the Serengeti—she retraced her flaps and stalked behind a Jitney leading her to a berthing place.

"Sleek looking mother, isn't she?" Chad bent down and yelled into Sarah's ear. "It's hard to think of someone not just having the money to buy one of those things, but also to be able to afford to keep it up."

Sarah plugged one of her ears to ward off the jet's screams. "I understand his father is some rich Chinese businessman?"

With a wry smile, Chad muttered, "I suppose what he does could be called business." Leaning to his left, he used his elbow and jabbed Peterr Manning in the arm. "Right, Peterr?"

The MiG had rolled to a stop and the engines were whining to a stop. "Well, whatever he does, it sure must pay well."

"You guys are just jealous…" Marissa Manning held her hand over her eyes and squinting at the MiG.

"Well, it's about time you're here…you're late. You didn't get to see the bird land." Peterr looked at his wife and made an approving face, "Why the uniform…want to impress someone, Captain?"

Without looking away from the plane, Marissa, mumbled, "Stow it, Mister." She raised her voice, "Hey, Sarah, there's your babysitter standing by the MiG?"

"Yeah…and of course, LT COL Blain…next to General Olmstead. I don't know the rest of that crowd."

"Don't look at me! Most of those guys must be from Pensacola…I've never seen them." Chad could feel the eyes on him. "I just came out to get a look at the MiG 31BM; I didn't know it was going to turn into a gathering of brass."

Peterr Manning gave a soft cough and tipped his head as he shot Chad a sly look. Turning his attention to the ladies he said, "Would you like to get a closer look at the bird? Maybe we can even get an intro to our mysterious guests."

"I'll say…is that little girl in the baggy flight suit his navigator?" Sarah chuckled, "I don't think sooo…more likely she hitched a joy ride with the infamous Ronald Chu."

"Yep, that's Ronald Chu, son of Miracle Chu and the girl is Victoria Rodrigo…her father was just assassinated in Caracas, Venezuela." Marissa Manning paused and returned the stares generated by her knowledge. "WHAT! Don't any of you guys listen to the news or the Air Police channels?"

"Sure we do, Sweetie, we just didn't know that *you* did." He looked at Chad and Sarah, "Well, she knew more than I did."

Sarah held her tongue, clenched her teeth and gave Marissa a questioning look out of the corner of her eyes.

Chad pursed his lips and said, "Well, good for you, Marissa." Turning to Sarah he said, "Would you ladies like to join us at the O Club…Colonel Blain has invited us to lunch with the guests."

"Anything new on Ronald Chu's father, Chad… or should I be asking Marissa?"

Peterrr erupted into a horse laugh. "I swear, Marissa, you are a wonder and a marvel…must be all of that rich rearing' you had."

The sudden tension in the air was suffocating. It was obvious something was really bothering Peterrr Manning. An awkward silence fell over the group.

Peterrr continued, "Bet you all didn't know 'Miss Got Rocks' here was from New England…she's an only child. She inherited her rich European family's money *and* her cousin's money…may she rest in peace." Peterr performed a mock "Sign of the Cross."

"Yep, filthy rich."

The air was saturated with feelings of embarrassment. "We better get going…we don't want to be late for the luncheon." Sarah grabbed Marissa by the arm, "You guys can meet us at the Club and we'll take Marissa's car." She leaned into Marissa and the two walked off as if they were two sorority sisters heading for the powder room.

Chad turned to Peterr, "I'll never understand women. What was all that about?" He was feeling uncomfortable and it showed.

"Haven't got a clue, 'cept Mar doesn't like me to mention her money and especially anything about her cousin, Heather." He shrugged and grabbed Chad's arm in a mock of the two girls. "Shall we?"

Chad winced and created a wrinkled face. There was something behind Peterr's sudden outburst, Chad had a feeling Sarah knew what it was. Since the first day she met Marissa, Sarah had been researching Marissa's past. Last week she had received a letter which must have tied things together because Sarah had suddenly stopped her inquires.

*   *   *

The first hour of the luncheon seemed more like a political fund raiser—Ronald and Victoria were "guests of honor" and treated like visiting monarchs. Besides the disappearance of his father and the qualities of the MiG-31BM, there were discreet questions about Victoria and Hector Rodrigo.

"Look, Gentlemen, I would love to allow you to check out the MiG, but my father has a strict agreement with the governments of China and Russia…no foreign *check outs*. I'm sure you understand." Ronald pasted on his most cordial smile. "You may look but not touch AND *no* inside photos."

"Just like your lovely friend, hey?" LT COL Blain looked about the table seeking the approval of his fellow officers. Quickly he shifted his attention to Victoria, "My Dear, how did you find Venezuela?"

Victoria tilted her head and gave the Colonel a quizzical look. "Why, Colonel…I didn't *find* it at all. It was just *there.*" She finished with a coquettish grin and listened as all of the men rewarded her humor with roaring guffaws.

When the laughter subsided, Ronald began speaking with a more somber tone. "Gentlemen, Miss Victoria was the prisoner of Hector Rodrigo since childhood. She was sold to him by some opportunistic American agency and is now well rid of him."

The abrupt silence at the table was unmistakable—everyone, but Ronald, was immediately made uncomfortable. The tension only lasted for a few seconds but seemed like an eternity.

A red faced Blain tipped his head, "I'm sorry, My Dear, I had no idea. Please forgive me."

In her most gracious tone, Victoria said, "Colonel…how could you know? The man was a pig and the world's well rid of him, but let's not speak about that." She grinned and raised her glass of red wine, "To America…your home, and mine. I hope to find a new life here, Gentlemen. Please be the first to welcome me back home."

She felt relieved. Hector was dead and she was in America, the land of her parents. Only one thing was missing…the cryptic announcement by Ronald, "Would you like to meet your mother's best friend?"

Turning her gaze to Ronald, her tears began to wash down her cheeks. "Thank you, Ronald…you have made a young girl's dreams come true." Victoria continued to look at Ronald while the other men chanted, "Welcome home, Victoria!"

At a nearby table, Chad and Sarah, Peterr and Marissa were occupied listening to the exchanges. Few words were being spoken at their table, for that matter little was going on at all—drinks were not being touched and the food was not being consumed.

"So, she's really an American. What a fascinating Cinderella story, a real Hollywood ending, wouldn't you say?" Peterr Manning could only shake his head and comment, "I wonder how she ended up in South America. I thought we were the country that brought children here, not sent some of ours abroad."

Sarah picked up her drink and took a slow swallow, "Bet the first thing she does is try to find her parents." Deliberately, she avoided eye contact with anyone at their table.

"Why do you think she'll do that?" Chad asked as he blinked his eyes and shook his head in a gesture of disbelief. "They abandoned her, Sarah, for heaven's sake."

Before Sarah could answer, Marissa interjected, "You don't know a thing, Chad. There might have been a good reason why her parents had to put her up for adoption."

"Yeah, Chad…things happen. If that had happened to me, I would want to find my roots and understand why I was rejected." Sarah paused and looked at the gaping mouths of the two men, "Honestly, sometimes I think you men have no sensitivity. She has had a tough life…now she wants to find out why."

"Okay, okay…we get it. Sorry, Sarah…Marissa. I didn't mean anything by it." Chad picked up his drink and looked at Peterr. He shrugged and made a face to match his confusion. Slowly, he sipped his wine while he looked around the table but when his eyes locked on Marissa's wet eyes his stomach clutched

Chapter 38

For the past two days the activity at the Microwave base seemed normal, but below ground there was a flurry of activity akin to a drowning ant colony. Three rows of computer operators were busily scanning, analyzing and reporting to another group of collators who, in turn, were feeding data to a remote site on the base.

"I don't understand how this thing got so far out of control." A crusty-looking Navy Admiral blurted out as he slammed down a stack of photos. The pictures landed on top of a report that reading, TOP SECRET, FOR YOUR EYES ONLY. "This was not supposed to happen." His large fingers pointed at a group of technicians who were cowering at a make-shift table.

In a defiant response, one of the ladies shot to her feet, "Sir, you have to understand…we only did as we were told.

We had no idea they would actually succeed in building the damn device." She disappeared quickly and dropped back into her seat.

"It's true, sir." A young major seated at the conference table looked at the Admiral. "We were told the purpose of the exercise was to get them to pour a fortune into TRYING to beat us in developing the Susame Project." He paused and looked down at the general seated next to him…the major seemed to be looking for support to his statement. Not getting any help, he continued, "It is still possible they are just bluffing…after all, we haven't seen it work."

Smashing his fist into the scattered papers, he yelled, "HAVEN"T SEEN IT WORK!! Are you absolutely, nuts, or just plain incompetent?" He took a deep breath and muttered to himself. "If Intel is right, they are going to TEST the damned thing right here…do you understand…right HERE! In a few days we won't have to wonder if it works…Jesus Christ, man!" He tossed the bundle of papers down the length of the conference table, scattering most on the table with the others gliding on the floor.

"They won't do that, Admiral." The voice came from the back of the room. It was distinctly a male voice, but it was coming from a part of the room deep in shadows. The man stepped forward and a sliver of light passed over the wrinkled face of LT COL Blain. "They are bluffing us, sir." He paused—it was obvious he was waiting for someone to ask why he so believed the tale.

The admiral bit, "Oh…and just why do you believe that, Colonel?" The tone was obviously one of distain.

For effect, Blain waited for the whispers to subside. "Because, sir…they don't really know we don't have the same device." He took another step forward, "I am not saying we should not pay them their blood money, but I am saying that, IF we do…THEY will believe we do not have a similar device and THEY will fire upon us."

A sly smile and a snort escaped from the admiral. "So you are suggesting we raise the ante. We bluff their bluff?'

"They might not be bluffing, Sir, but I am betting we have a real 'ace in the hole,' sir."

"What is that, Colonel?"

This time the Colonel stepped so that he was fully into the light. "We have the son of

Miracle Chu…right here on the base." The room filled with an undercurrent of whispers. "Miracle Chu is reputed to be the negotiator, sponsor and treasurer of the overseas Susame consortium". More muttering erupted, "He is on his way to Florida to join his son. I think, as long as they are here…the freighter will not risk testing the device."

 "Or they will choose a different target…like Washington." The defiant woman was again on her feet. "You will have to admit, Colonel, there is nothing to stop them from firing on…say, the Pensacola U. S. Naval Base!"

Blain threw his hands open in a gesture indicating he considered it a possibility. "That is why I think it is in our best interest to pay them off…for now." He raised his hands to quell the murrers, "BUT, when Miracle Chu and his son are here…we should raid the freighter and make sure we are in no danger."

"And if the device is real…you plan to steal it, Colonel?"

"Acquire, Captain Manning…acquire."

Captain Marissa Manning shook her head in disbelief. "That's a long shot, Colonel. What happens if you're wrong?"

"I'm not, Captain. I'm not wrong… At any rate, I don't think we have a lot of options." The Colonel moved to a nearby seat and sat down as if to say "that is that." He folded his arms and moved his eyes about the room like some robot acquiring the next target for its death ray.

Marissa raised her voice and deliberately avoided eye contact with the smoldering Colonel. "Admiral…?"

"Yes, Captain." The Adriral had begun to pool his papers together—a sure sign he was about to close the session. "Well, what is it?"

With balled fists at her sides, she almost shouted, "Sir, I believe there is another option open to us."

Blain muttered, "Of course you do."

Holding up his hand in a gesture of silence, the Admiral turned his face toward the eight scientists and technicians. "How close are we to having our own Susame device?"

The entire room fell into a hush suitable for a deserted New Orleans mausoleum. The group began looking at one another—

eyes were cast down and heads rolled from one side to another. Finally, the one other woman among them, a scientist, said, "Admiral…we are not the only group assigned to this project."

With an impatient bite in his tone, the Admiral released his words

"Please…answer…the question." He paused, "Miss—"

"Our assignment was to *appear* to have the weapon…not to *actually* do R & D then develop one real-time. As you know, we consider the development of such a devastating tool as unconscionable. Even the energy project would take years to produce a working model." She lowered her voice and murmured, "If not impossible to make, much less to control."

Slowly, the Admiral stood up and looked at the other officers seated at the conference table. "Gentlemen, Ladies, did you hear that?" Next he turned his head and stared at the bewildered scientists. His voice moved up half an octave and he shouted, "Then why in the hell do all of these reports…" he stopped speaking and scattered the papers he had just stacked, "show such glowing progress, and I might add, such massive expenditures? Let me put it another damned way, what was all this money used for if not…?"

Unruffled, the woman responded, "The documents were meant to be found and sold in order to give plausibility to the project…it was our hope that Major Buford would be taken by either the Chinese or the South Americans. Under torture he would have substantiated what he believed to be true." She glanced toward Captain Marissa Manning, but Marissa showed no reaction. "It's not that unusual a tactic, sir. You know…let the other guy spend all of the money to develop the product and we buy the results from one of our double agents."

All the Admiral could do was grumble. It was true, and not the first time that such subterfuge was used but they seldom succeeded for any length of time. Maybe length of time was not important in this case—he didn't know because this was just one of those assignments handed out because he was in a particular place at the wrong time. "Captain?"

Marissa snapped out of her thoughts and her training took over. She knew how things worked—for years she had worked with people like Chad and Peterr while they did their intelligence work. As far as anyone knew, she had not had any actual field experience. "Yes, sir?"

He was trying to calm down, but there was still a distinct edge to his voice, "What do you want to say?" He had begun reorganizing his papers.

"Intel shows Miracle Chu will be here very soon. I would like to recommend we meet with Miracle and his son, Ronald, to discuss another way of getting out of this mess…sir."

"What makes you think they would meet with us?" The Admiral looked about the room as if seeking some enlightenment to his question.

"Maybe they won't, but there is always the option of taking them into custody while we raid the freighter. Call it 'our ace in the hole,' or just Yankee leverage, sir, but if we can get on that freighter…we can capture the device. That is, of course, if it really exists."

At that point the officers at the table went into a huddle and whispered for the next two minutes. Occasionally, a voice would rise and sometimes an expletive would escape but for the most part they were indiscernible.

Marissa looked at Blain and wondered how much he really knew about the project. His daughter had done babysitting for both her and Sarah Buford…had they been spying on her? Even her husband did not know of her association with the Susame Project…at least she didn't *think* he knew. There were other things on her mind besides all the political posturing—she didn't think anyone would wildly imagine using it as an offensive weapon, but then this would not be the first time she had come up with a wrong conclusion.

"Captain…we might need to use your husband…any problems?" The Admiral folded his arms and tipped his chin as he waited for her response.

"Use…what do you mean 'use?'" Her head cocked to one side as she narrowed her eyes.

Pasting an affable smile on his face the Admiral glanced about his circle of officers, "Just an expression, Captain…would you prefer the words, 'need his help?'"

"'Help' would be fine, sir." Marissa knew the Admiral had changed the semantics but still meant to *use* her husband. Her reputation as a cold-hearted bitch just might cost the life of Peterr Manning.

Chapter 39

Miracle Chu watched the sun peek over the eastern horizon, his thoughts not the usual reflections of a person witnessing the habitual ritual—today, only the ugly face of an indifferent murderer.

"Pretty, huh?" The ship's captain gave the wheel a gentle nudge as he adjusted the course of the chartered fishing boat. "Don't like the 'red sky' out there…you know the old saying, 'red sky at morning, sailor take warning.' Well, it's true…yes, sir, true enough." He nudged his throttles forward and the boat growled like a wounded hippopotamus—deep and throaty. "Yep…sometimes they just come out of nowhere and move off just as fast."

On the advice of his friend in Barranquilla, Columbia, Miracle had his friend charter a marlin fishing boat to take him to Kingston, Jamaica. He was traveling under the somewhat ridiculous pseudonym of Mr. Smith. Miracle glanced at his watch, "Are you expecting bad weather?"

The middle age 'captain' squinted his sun-browned eyelids, "Hard to tell…one minute it's like a mountain lake and the next you would swear God himself was out to sink 'ya.'" For the next ten minutes the man reeled off stories of storms that sunk other boats and ships, some with all hands lost.

As the man continued his sea yarns of the Bermuda Triangle, Miracle found it hard to take his eyes off the ascending sun. For the thousandth time he struggled with the morality of the Susame Project. Was it really possible the benevolent ball of fire which sustains life on the earth could be used as a weapon to kill people, devastate cities, even whole nations, or possibly the whole planet? Why the weapon in the first place? The energy program was just as controlling and it benefited mankind. Even now, his son was in danger of being killed. Again he glanced at his watch, "When do you expect to be in port?"

The boat captain paused and pushed out his lips as he thought out loud. "Well, we're making good time, about twenty knots, but you know we're not a speed boat." He bounced his head from one side to the other and said, "Ah…about noon we should be nearing Kingston." For the first time the seaman asked a question, "Whatcha gonna do there, Mister…Smith?"

Miracle snickered, "Fish…what else?"

The two men laughed and then fell into a mutual silence.

Miracle was certain his chartered seaplane would wait for him. *God knows I'm paying him enough.* It was crucial he arrive at the freighter in time to stop…no, *postpone* the test. In his communication with the freighter he was unable to convince them he was really Miracle Chu, he would have to show himself if he wanted to discuss anything concerning the scheduled start.

Abruptly, the silence was broken, "I'm putting the boat on auto-pilot…you want some coffee?"

"Yes, please…" In the back of Miracle's mind he recalled the way he was drugged while on his private jet. "I'll go with you. I could use a change of view."

"Okay with me, but one of us ought to keep an eye out for pirates. There're not a lot of them here, but you never know." He shrugged as if he had just gone through the kind of announcements given by airline personal.

Miracle smiled, "I'd be glad to get us both some coffee…black?"

The boatman nodded.

Miracle began heading for the galley, he also took note of the possibility he could pilot the boat without this 'captain'. With the auto-pilot set for Kingston, he at least had an option. It was the first time he noticed the boat was picking up some larger waves—like a metal pinball, he was pitched around the tiny gangway as he worked his way aft. It seemed the sea had a much stronger effect on him than when he was young and visiting relatives in China. Among the myriad smells erupting from below deck, he managed to track down a fancy Gevalia twelve pot brewer that was so clean it looked out of place with all of the other well-aged utensils. After rinsing out two blue porcelain cups, Miracle oozed the dark brew into the cups then bounced his way back up to the bridge, periodically cussing as the hot coffee splashed out onto his hands.

Still holding on to the wheel, the captain stared out to sea—he resembled the wax figures that Miracle had seen at a museum in London, England. "Yep, just what I feared, that damned wind is pushing' down from the northwest…nothing in Florida or Jamaica to stop it, too damned flat." He reached for the coffee mug and dipped his head to indicate heart-felt appreciation. "It won't be long before we'll be like a toothpick in a washing machine, my friend."

Carefully, he watched to see if the captain really drank his coffee—Miracle hated he had to live his life wondering if his next drink would be his last. "What are you saying, Captain?"

He waved his cup around as he spoke; bits of black coffee dribbled down the side and fell among thousands of other marks on the wooden deck. "Not likely that we'll be in Kingston on time, Mister Smith." The fishing boat was beginning to dip and pitch in the oncoming swells. "Good thing we can head into the waves, but your plane will have a hell of a time taking off if this weather continues."

Miracle's eyebrows moved together—he wasn't sure if he should say anything, but he could not recall telling the captain he was going to catch a plane at Kingston. If there was something untoward, he decided it was best to not tip his hand. "I see you have a new coffee pot…at least it looks new."

"Yeah, nice…a little too fancy for my taste, but my girlfriend insisted … if I was going to pilot some 'big shot' all this way I should at least have a better coffee pot…she bought it for me." The captain laughed and reached inside a cubby hole next to his steering wheel. "Want me to sweeten up that drink, Mr. Smith?" He held up an amber bottle, half full of Old Crow whiskey.

The elderly Chinese held up his hand to indicate he would pass on the offer. He watched as the sea faring pilot whipped the bottle to his lips and took a big swallow—then the captain poured a generous amount into his own cup.

After slipping the bottle back into the cubby hole, he shook his head to indicate his approval. "Great stuff…settles my stomach and steadies the nerves, you know." Then he took a sip from his coffee cup and smiled, "Sure you won't join me?"

His head wagged, not so much that he disapproved of the drink but because he was concerned… No, he was worried he would not get to the Gulf of Mexico in time to stop them from running the test on Eglin Air Force Base…Ronald would surely be killed. He had to find a way to warn him, that much was certain. "Where is your ship-to-shore link?"

"She's below, but I'm not sure you can reach anyone out here…at least not anyone you want to meet. Police, Coast Guard, Cubans, and Pirates all monitor those channels." He shrugged, "If I was you…I'd think about it, and…I'm not too keen on ending up dead or in a Cuban jail." He tipped his head to one side, indicating he was waiting for an agreement from Miracle Chu.

Forced to reply with a fake grin, Miracle shrugged and asked, "Well, what would you do if you had a problem out here?"

The captain feigned the pain of deep thinking and then burst into laughter, "Probably sink!" He seemed so amused with himself he continued to grunt, chuckle, and mutter under his breath, *Sink, sink, sink…*

"How about a cell phone?"

"When they can, they listen to those too. The bastards are everywhere, Mister

Smith…don't you know that?" His tone was almost belligerent.

Miracle was never a man to just lie down and give up…there had to be a way. "Give me your cell—" It wasn't a request, the words fell out of his mouth just the same way they had bitten into the souls of hundreds of men. "I must call Florida."

The captain was confused; the tone of the man speaking to him had a ring which touched a chord somewhere inside his body…it was fear, the fear that comes from knowledge of end-time events. This man was to be feared, no doubt. At first impression, he looked like an old and helpless elderly citizen, but, suddenly, he was like a stalking tiger, ready to devour anyone who stood in his way.

He reached in his pocket and pulled out a purple phone and sheepishly said, "It's my girlfriend's." He held it out to Miracle, "I'm not sure you can get anything out here."

"Miracle smiled, we'll see." He remembered a movie about the Second World War, *Wind Talkers* with Nicholas Cage. The story was about how the Navaho Indians would speak on the walkie-talkies to one another using their native language…it turned out to be an unbreakable code. Miracle would talk to Ronald in one of the obscure dialects of provincial China.

Chapter 40

With a violent shove of the computer mouse, Barnacle glared at the computer screen, taken aback and rubbing the sides of his face. *So the report's true.* "Damn it…! The old Chinaman's still alive!" After a quick breath, Barnacle shrugged and changed his tone, "Well, at any rate, he is going to be in Florida. This time I will take care of it myself." *I'm not going to risk that, someday, he could testify against me.*

Since the beginning of the Susame plan, Barnacle had no intention of sharing the enormous wealth gained from it, but even more, Barnacle had wanted the power all to himself. The major problem would be how to wield the power and still remain anonymous…maybe he couldn't succeed in doing that but maybe it didn't matter. So far, agents working for Barnacle had been able to gather the information he used to control others—if this would work in the future, only time would tell.

Before tomorrow was over, Barnacle would be hailed as a national hero, no…THE national hero—that was a major part of the new plan, but it had become vital no one ever know his real identity. Only a few of his associates knew his real intent. It was a test…but not what they thought.

Using a scramble phone, he routed a call through the freighter still waiting at anchor just off of the west coast of Florida. "I want it clearly understood…I will tell you when we are ready for the show."

There was no hesitation in the voice at the other end of the line, "Yes?"

"There is to be NO testing until I give the word…there are crucial issues at play here. If you wish to survive, you will need to follow my instructions to the letter. Is that understood?" Barnacle heard a gasp at the other end of the line then said, "You have a problem with that?"

She stifled the gulp in her throat, "Of course not." Getting herself out of the blast area would be easy enough, but what about those whom she loved? "Are you sure about the anticipated blast area?"

Barnacle chuckled, "Well…if it isn't right I'd be in serious trouble…wouldn't I?" There was a pause on the line. "We'll see each other again, later." The scramble phone went dead.

For a moment Marissa held the phone and looked at it with confusion. Barnacle hadn't indicated they had seen each other before…and *what* meeting? The only scheduled meeting had been at the base to welcome Miracle Chu. She thought a moment then surmised… *Could Barnacle have been one of the people at THE meeting?* Her mind reeled with possibilities—for all she knew; Barnacle could be part of the refueling crew or a tower operator. Just the idea she had been in contact with Barnacle was a big break through.

Sarah heard the garage door open—Peterr was coming back from the base and she would have to pass the information on to him…he would be thrilled—Barnacle might have been at the base today.

As the door opened, Peterr grinned at her, "Guess who I brought home with me?"

Marissa felt breathless. Standing alongside Peterrr were Ronald Chu and the ward of Hector Rodrigo, Victoria Rodrigo. She wanted to speak but was afraid to open her mouth and reveal more than she cared to at the moment—she put out her hand and nodded.

"They wanted to meet you, Marissa." He hesitated and looked at her, trying to read her demeanor. "Are you all right, Marring?"

"Yeah, sure, just…really…surprised." A smile pasted on her face, she looked at the young couple and said, "Well, you two have had quite the adventure." Turning to Ronald she added, "We were all pleased to hear your father is all right. Have you heard from him?"

The atmosphere in the kitchen seemed stiff and a bit tense. Ronald ignored Marissa's question.

"Let's go into the living room. Would either of you like something to drink?" Peterr was doing his best to be the cordial host but already he was beginning to think thoughts only Marissa could answer. He didn't like what he was thinking.

Sarah could not help but feel a bit awkward. She had something to tell Peterr. It was of great urgency, but now two celebrity guests had arrived. *Good thing the kids aren't home yet.* "I'm sorry. I'm just bothered by all that's happened." Turning to Peterr she mumbled, "The kids are with Hillary and Uncle Blainy—" Noticing her guests were looking at her, she said, "She's LT COL Blain's daughter…she often babysits for us. The kids call the Colonel 'Uncle Blainy' and really love him. " Abruptly, she turned to Ronald, "You never answered my question."

"What was that?" Ronald Chu and Victoria sat down and exchanged questioning looks.

Marissa wrinkled her forehead, "Your father… Have you heard from him?"

Ronald politely shrugged. "I believe he's well, but I don't know where he is…at least not at the moment." They held out hands and took the drinks Peterr had gotten. "He is a very cautious man, Mrs. Manning…it is likely he's avoiding anyone putting some kind of trace on him."

"Then you don't think the plane crash was an accident?" Peterr sat on the arm of Marissa's overstuffed chair. He ignored her disapproving eyes.

Victoria took the pause to answer Peterr's question, "It was probably done by

Hector…I heard him talking to a person he called, 'Barnacle'…the voice sounded funny, like maybe it was filtered."

It was an involuntary look, but both Marissa and Peterr exchanged glances. "We've heard that name, Victoria."

Vicroia continued, "He told Hector to make sure some package was put on the plane. I think they did not want Mr. Chu to reach Cuba." She reached over and held Ronald's hand, "We talked about it on our way here." Looking up at Ronald she said, "Mr. Manning, I think Ronald knows more than he told me…maybe he will talk to you two."

"Well, Ronald?" Marissa leaned forward. "Maybe he doesn't want to discuss it, Darling." Peterr spoke softly, trying to avoid getting her stirred up.

Ronald nodded, and then moved his eyes about the room. "It's family stuff. Thank you for your interest, but that is not why I wanted her to meet you." He turned his attention to Victoria.

There was a moment of tension in the room, like the way people study the sky when black clouds are gathering and lightning is about to strike the earth.

"Victoria…this lady knows who your mother is. Marissa Manning is the cousin of your mother, Victoria. She's your aunt." He watched as Victoria searched her feelings. "And…I think she knows where your mother is."

Peterr Manning did not move one muscle—he sat on the arm rest and looked at Victoria, then Marissa. Finally, he broke the silence. "What makes you think a crazy thing like that, Ronald?" Peterrr's face had blanched, not anger, but confusion.

Ronald wanted to answer, but he was waiting…waiting for Marissa or Victoria to say something. "My father's rich, Peterrr…and he knows people."

By now, Victoria was shaking with expectaions, her mind reeling. She had not taken Ronald's words scriously when he had asked her if she would like to meet a friend of her mother. She could feel her mouth speaking…her heart pounded. "Is he right? Do you know my mother?" The full force of her hand was crushing Ronald's fingers, her brow wrinkled.

Her nostrils and chest shuddered as her eyes clouded over. Marissa gave a quick look at the stunned face of Peterr Manning.

"Yes, Victoria…it's true, I knew your mother. Her name was Heather DeVunder…same as my maiden name. I too was a DeVunder. Her father was my dad's brother. We lived in Europe. At the time, Heather was living in the United States." Marissa had wanted to call her *Dear,* but the words stuck in her throat. How could this young girl ever understand the hell Heather had gone through ever since that night when her parents literally tore the child from Heather's arms and enforced their decision? "She was my…cousin."

There was shock in Peterrr's voice when he said, "You've never really talked about your cousin, Marissa."

"And who was Vicky's father?" Ronald turned his gaze to Marissa, "Will you tell Victoria?" His words were chilly and lacked any form of human compassion— flat, mechanical.

By now, Victoria's face was white, drained as the blood moved from her head. The room began to spin as she slumped to her side and draped her weak body across Ronald's lap. She let out a soft sigh as she slipped into unconsciousness. Only one word escaped from her pale lips, "Why?"

Both Peterrr and Marissa stepped over to Victoria, who had passed out.

"What happened?" Peterr, who was used to dealing with every sort of crisis, felt helpless. *Who was this girl? Where had she come from? Why hadn't Marissa told him about her? What did Marissa know about the father of her mysterious niece?*

Marissa knelt at Victoria's side and stoked the forehead of the young girl. Victoria seemed so young, so fragile, yet there seemed to be a stiffness about her that seemed advanced for her years. Questions whirred through Marissa's mind, they wouldn't settle fast enough to wrestle with answers. "She's passed out; I think…the moment seemed just too much for her." Marissa dabbed at the tears that were blurring her vision and bleeding colors down from her cosmetic decorated eyes.

"She needs to rest—" Ronald had not known what to expect but was not prepared to have Victoria pass out before his eyes. He was concerned, but not worried…she was a fighter. To Ronald, this was the best way to tell her…now he began to reconsider. *Maybe it's different with women.* Ronald could sense the tension between Marissa and

Peterr Manning; no doubt Peterrr didn't like Ronald's timing with *the bombshell.*

The announcement Victoria was her niece was no revelation to Marissa. Her wealthy parents made sure the illegitimate child was disposed of before the event could sully the family name, typical of the well-to-do. It was at a prestigious orphanage that Hector found the pretty young girl—to him, it was like discovering a budding rose among a field of dandelions. Later, when Marissa had joined military intelligence, she tracked down the girl. Daily, it pained her that Victoria was not growing up with children like Carl and Betsy. Now, here, Victoria could…and Marissa feared the pain she had avoided years ago had come to fruition. Victoria was here, Peterr would have to be told the whole story, and time when a mad man might be preparing to blow a piece of Florida off the map…all she could think about was the obvious—would her marriage survive? Would Victoria ever heal?

Chapter 41

Without success, Miracle had tried to call Ronald, but getting a solid signal on the cell proved impossible. The seas were rolling in with six foot swells, and they were not yet close enough to land to connect to any coastal signal tower—and it might get worse as they approached landfall. He was feeling trapped, frustrated and angry. "I can't get anyone…just no signal!" He yelled in the captain's ear. It took three times before he could be heard over the noise of the engines, the wipers blades, and slapping sounds made by the waves striking the boat.

Keeping his eyes on the incoming waves, the captain shouted, "You'll have to try the ship-to-shore…it's tied into a GPS system, but the other end will need a good receiver." The captain sounded breathless—it was obvious he was fearful. "I haven't seen it this bad since…well, I can't remember, Mr.—"
Miracle steadied against the cabin bulkhead and considered the situation—if he used the ship-to-shore he stood a good chance of being located as well as overheard…but would have to change it. "Okay!" he nodded and headed below to use the transmitter. The trip down the stairwell

was only a short distance, but he was banged about like a billiard ball bouncing off the rails.

The transmitter was already powered up; a precaution the captain had taken in case of an emergency. Miracle Chu could not get a connection to Ronald's cell. In quiet despair he leaned back against the soiled cushions of a bolted down chair and lowered his shoulders in resignation of the situation…he would not be able to save Ronald. Scenes flashed thought his mind, pictures of events flooded past his inner eye as he lamented— how hard Ronald had tried to save him.

"Any success?" the captain yelled though his speaker system.

"Can't raise them…I'll try later." A revelation pierced his consciousness, but he could not grasp it—an idea, a solution. Involuntarily, his face began to relax, his mouth fell open. Of course…the MiG! The MiG had a satellite link and a powerful receiver always on. He could transmit to the MiG and it would relay to Ronald's cell phone…IF Ronald had remembered to open the link.

"I think I have a way, captain!" Miracle wanted to shout, to tell everyone, to share the good news—he might be able to save his son.

"Good" was all the captain could manage to say.

With renewed enthusiasm, Miracle entered the settings for the link with the special satellite and smiled as he heard it connect. Next he linked to the MiG31 and entered his access code. As a voice speaking in Mandarin Chinese responded, "You are being recorded…speak now." Quickly, Miracle switched to a provincial dialect and reported the circumstances to Ronald, ending by telling him to evacuate immediately and not to worry about him. Now that the message had been sent, he petitioned his ancestors to intercede and make sure Ronald received the message in time.

"Put it back on the American Coast Guard frequency!" the captain said. "There's a big one coming in…hold on!"

The boat shuddered as it struggled to climb the curving wall of water. For a moment, everything seemed to suspend in time—the curl of the wave hung just above the deck of the fishing boat while the boat resembled a stick-on photo pasted on a nautical scene. With the force of a fire hose hitting concrete, the wall of water crashed over the bow—the force ripped loose cable riggings. The v-shape of the bow split some of the wave to the side, only to be catapulted onto the stern of the boat.

On the back side of the wave, they dipped into a shallow trough. Through the intercom, the captain's shaky voice remarked, "A good one, huh?" Audibly, he swallowed, "Looks better ahead…can you take the wheel while I check the damage?"

The violence of the wave had thrown Miracle about the lower cab. First he hit the leg of the folding table and then was tossed into a roll that bounced him between the leg and a bolted-down chair. A thin trail of blood leaked into his left eye as he struggled to right himself. He was feeling weak and his lower back sent sharp pains up his spine. Miracle was no stranger to rough water, but this time he had been preoccupied and neglected to hold on to a safe place. He could not allow himself to admit his age might also be a factor. Wincing with pain, he reached the mike—ignoring the ache, he took several deep breaths. "I got knocked about…a bit, but I think I can…help…out."

"Get your message off?" The captain's tone was like someone asking him if he had his cereal that morning.

"Yes…thanks." Miracle forced out a feeble response. "I reset the frequency too." He was now inching his body into the chair that had pounded him with the vicious temperament of a lead pipe.

The wall speaker crackled again, "I use the American Coast Guard settings because the Cuban base at Guantanamo Bay talks to them…in case you're wondering." Hearing no response, he added, "They're less than two hundred miles from Kingston…you okay?"

"Be right there." Miracle dabbed at the gash above his left eyebrow. He fought off his light headedness and staggered toward the steps that would take him to the bridge. *I hope Ronald got my message.* "Ronald, if you can hear me, check the MiG."

Step by step, he began pulling his wounded body up the stairs in the tight passageway. For one of the only times in his life he was feeling old…older than his years, just wanting to rest. He sat on one of the steps and waited for the ringing in his ears and the dizzy-sick feeling to pass.

Chapter 42

Time was running out--Barnacle grew more angry every second. *The damn Chink,* he thought, *is causing delays!* With time, Barnacle was certain he would be able to track down all of the money Miracle had stashed away, but right now, Barnacle most resented the interference. Delaying the test was not really a problem, but forcing the high and mighty United States of America to pay…well, that would "make Barnacle's day." If Miracle Chu had pulled off another one of his miracles, well, maybe, just maybe, Barnacle could use the situation to his advantage—a call to the freighter should do it.

The man looked down at the scrambler. He had not been expecting any calls this close to test time. "Now, what do you want?" The voice was gruff and filled with irritation.

For a few seconds, Barnacle could feel anger zipping through his tensed muscles. Quickly Barnacle calmed down. "I have just learned that Miracle Chu has survived his…misadventure in Columbia. It is my belief he is coming to see you."

"We heard from him…at least we think it *might* be him." There was a three second pause on the line, "He wants us to delay announcing the launch until he arrives."

Barnacle's ears perked up. "You know where he is?" Even the scrambler could not hide his sudden interest—he could still accomplish his plan to get rid of the old Chinaman, but there was still the money.

"Not really, well, sort of. We had him pegged as being North East of Columbia, SA, but he could have been on a plane…or a boat. Hell, he could have really even been playing with us and be berthed alongside." He broke out in a chuckle, "You know how it works when people route themselves from all over the world."

"Did he say *when* he would be at the freighter? How soon?" Barnacle could feel the surge in his veins…the thrill of the hunt. There was still a chance he could…

By now the seaman was beginning to wonder what was going on, he knew both Barnacle and Miracle Chu kept him in the dark, but this was something new. This was a power grab and he was going to be caught in the middle. Do you go with the *money man* or the *boss man?* "He wants us to delay the test…he said late afternoon."

That would put him at some distance, and headed for Florida. "He probably wants to save his son, Ronald." Barnacle paused, "If he calls back, try to pinpoint him…and…tell him you agree to delay the testing."

"But…but…!"

"I said, *'Tell* him you agree.' I did not say that we should *actually* delay the test." Barnacle waited for his words to sink in. "Proceed as planned!" Again he paused, "You *do* remember the plan, don't you?"

"Of course…is everything prepared at your end, Barnacle?"

"Most certainly…don't worry about me. You'll get your money…cash on delivery." The line went dead as Barnacle slowly lowered the receiver into its cradle. His only unfinished business was Miracle Chu…he was the only one who could ruin the day. Barnacle checked an eagle-faced wristwatch. It was almost time to set things in motion. Barnacle read the inscription, *Money is ephemeral—Power is forever.* Picking up a desk phone, Barnacle snarled, "Bring me that Susame file!"

Barnacle felt an increase in heart rate as he considered the future. There would be wealth, but much more than that, he would have the power he so richly deserved—the power denied him just because he was not born of New England blue blood. He would have total command, not of some small military group, but of a nation…the most powerful nation on the earth—and he meant to rule it with a fist of titanium.

Chapter 43

Like a crawling insect, Ronald's cell phone vibrated across the surface of the Manning coffee table—buzzing and dancing as if enjoying the moment. When it reached the edge of the table it whirled and slid until it dropped to the carpet below—there it rested, resembling a discarded Christmas toy…

In the bedroom of Peterr and Marissa Manning, Victoria was recovering from news revealed by Ronald and the Mannings, stretched out like Snow White waiting for the kiss from her hero prince as she began to open her eyes. Reluctant to move any other part of her body, her eyes moved about the room. "Where am I?" For a brief instant she feared she was back in Caracas and in one of Hector's secret rooms about to be part of another sadistic game.

"You fainted, Victoria." Marissa Manning sat on the edge of the bed and picked up Victoria's hand. A flood of thoughts raced through her brain, but all she could think to say was, "We have two children, Victoria." She paused to give Victoria a motherly smile, "They'll be home soon, Dear."

He had wanted to call her "Victoria" but Peterr Manning did not know what to do. Who was this young girl and, more to the point, who was the father of Marissa's cousin's child? Why hadn't Marissa told him about her…then, again, had he told Marissa about all of his early life? For that matter, he was beginning to believe he didn't really know who Marissa was—he had thought she had become a drunk only to discover that, sometime, she might have been faking it. Now there was the revelation concerning Victoria Rodrigo…or whatever the last name. Peterr had to say something before his insides exploded from all of the anxiety. "Victoria—you are how old?"

Simple mathematics would answer the question.

Ronald was slow to pick up the meaning and Marissa wasn't sure—he could just be checking if she was coherent, but he could also be ascertaining the time of Victoria's conception. Marissa remained silent.

Confused, Victoria's eyebrows lowered and looked at the stranger who suddenly had an interest in her birthday—did he think she wanted a party? "Ah…they tell me I am nineteen. My adoption papers say as much." She reached out to Ronald…he was her only touch with reality, a connection with the past. "I have my papers in Ronald's plane. Hector kept them hidden from me, but I found them…I didn't have time to really look at all of them."

Juggling the numbers, he quickly subtracted Victoria's age of nineteen from Marissa's age of thirty-five. Marissa would have been sixteen at the time of Victoria's birth—long before Peterr Manning had even heard of the heiress from Pittsburg, Pennsylvania. Pregnant at fifteen and only a sophomore in high school would have been a disgrace to her wealthy family and there would have been an easy trace—he had found none. "Was your cousin, Heather, your same age and pregnant at fifteen?" Peterr wasn't as much shocked by the possibility as he was curious.

Without taking her eyes off Victoria, she responded to Peterr with the flat phrase, "Yes…she was pregnant at fifteen. When she visited me in Europe she told me all about the ill-fated affair." Marissa turned her head to face Peterr Manning. "She was a young, stupid girl, who was mad about her American boyfriend. Just after Victoria was born, Heather and I were riding two of our very spirited horses…a pair of darting foxes spooked the horses." Marissa paused to catch her breath and compose herself. "Heather died, and I was in the hospital for a long time." She signed and covered her eyes, "I still feel responsible for her death…we shouldn't have been riding, but I had insisted. It was my fault we were out there—"

"Heather was in love with this man? He couldn't have been a good person…he didn't even call or write to Heather…he showed no interest in her pregnancy."

Peterr was confused, not only by her story, but by the resulting tragedy for Victoria and Marissa.

Ronald and Victoria just exchanged looks. Ronald could barely follow what Marissa was saying but realized Victoria had the right time of her birth—August, 20, 1988. His investigators had done a meticulous search…Marissa had left out some of the facts.

For Victoria, there was only the question of why…why had her mother abandoned her? Now she knew part of the story…her mother was dead. Victoria also realized she had probably been acting on a dose of bad information about who her mother was…information certainly creating a dilemma.

Abruptly, Marissa stood up and began pacing—her strides short, her face painted with anger. "Look! It happened a long time ago. He was an American, and not in Europe. The revelation of her indiscretion would have damaged both American families' social status." She narrowed her eyes and looked at Peterr, "He's dead, Peterr. He died just before Heather went to Europe…he was ice skating and, they say he fell through thin ice." She dabbed at her eyes and muttered, "There was an inquiry."

"Then who's my father?" Victoria's voice erupted with a strange sound…soft and almost lilting. The words seemed to float in the air like a tiny hummingbird resting on the pedals of a pastel flower. "You said you knew *when* it happened, so my mother must have told you *who.*" Victoria sat up and dangled her feet over the edge of the bed. The movement made her lightheaded.

Marissa returned to the bed and sat down next to Victoria, holding the girl's hand as if seeking some strength from it. "Heather was just fifteen…dating an older boy who had just started graduate school at Penn State." She paused, "They fooled around a bit, but only a few times had they ever done anything serious." She paused and took a deep breath, looked at Peterr Manning and said, "She was dating, Chad Buford's brother, Charles. She was fifteen and he was almost twenty-three."

Peterr jumped in, "Charles Buford is her father?" He could feel the blood surge into his neck. "You never let on you knew *Chad* Buford. Does Chad know about her?"

"No…and I didn't really know Chad, and NO he doesn't know about Victoria. That was almost twenty years ago and his brother is dead. My cousin knew Charles and *she* knew Chad, but she seldom talked about Chad. Heather was from the United Sates, and she knew lots of people in that social circle—" Marissa was surprised she was beginning to feel some relief as she unburdened her lifelong secrets. "I only came to the United States to live with my uncle after my parents died in the Lockerby terrorist airline crash. My scars were not yet fully healed."

At her last remark, Peterr could only rub his face with the palms of his hands—he was breathing fast and feeling a rising in blood pressure. Chad Buford had never even hinted he knew that Marissa was the cousin of Charles' ex-girlfriend. Maybe he didn't know, but that was unlikely.

Victoria gasped and muttered, "You said Charles was my father." She looked at Marissa and waited for a response.

"Yes…he died in a tragic skating accident, but some suspected foul play." Marissa swallowed and took a deep breath. "Heather told him she was pregnant, but he told her to…*get rid of it.* He was going to give her money for the abortion.”

“So my father is…was Charles Buford, and NOT Chad Buford.” Victoria flushed, “OH…no!” She began to cry. “Oh, no, I’m so ashamed…oh, no.”

“What is it, Vicky?” Ronald moved in front of her and dropped to his knees, “What’s wrong?” He waited, but Victoria’s composure was shattered…she began to sob uncontrollably. “I think I’ve done something awful.”

Marissa looked at Victoria but Victoria continued to hide her face, sobs of anguish interrupting fits of anger.

Reflecting on what she had just said, Marissa could not imagine what had set the young girl off. “What…what, did I say something?”

Her voice cracked as she mumbled through her hands, “I thought…that…*she* was…my…mother.”

“She…who?” Peterr asked.

“Sarah…Sarah Buford.” Victoria removed her hands from her face. “Buford…Buford! One time when Hector was drunk, he let me glance at my birth certificate—my real last…name was…Buford. He said Buford…then something about Fort Walton Beach." She wiped her eyes with the back of her hands. "The birth certificate had said CHAS, for Charles and not CHAD, for Chad Buford…the handwriting was in blurred ink." Victoria searched the faces for understanding, "I thought, if Chad was my father, then Sarah was my mother. I didn't see my mother's maiden name."

The room went silent, only the sound of the battery operated wall clock ticked off the seconds with a steady, *click, click, click.*

"The adoption agency must have given Hector the birth information which Heather's mother provided." Marissa sighed, "She knew Heather was dating Charles Buford…auntie did not even want to discuss the issue. Charles' and Chad's family, like ours, was pretty well off…wealthy and socially connected…my aunt must have insisted the Buford name be on the certificate, not *father unknown.* " Moving her eyes from face to face, Marissa settled on Peterr's…"Heather wasn't that kind of girl. It's just that she couldn't let anyone know the truth."

Compassionately, Peterr explored Marissa's face, "Are you sure the real father wasn't a family member?"

"For God's sake! No, Peterr! He had passed on before that and, besides, he was a wonderful man. Perhaps his loss caused her to get involved with Charles…I don't really know."

Peterr paused, "Well, then, what did Chad think of the whole thing?"

"When my aunt found out, Heather was already three months along. She 'went on vacation' to Europe. Heather and my aunt were with us for a year, so none of her friends, or Chad, would have known Heather was pregnant or had a child. I'm sure some suspected but no one said anything when I came to the States." Marissa was feeling better now. The secret she had been carrying in her tortured mind was eking out. "I have struggled with the guilt of Heather's death…and the way things turned out for you, Victoria. It happened and there was nothing I could do until now."

Victoria shook her head in consternation. "I have been using Hector's phone to call Sarah Buford. I called her horrible names and accused her of unnamed crimes. I wanted her to suffer like I have." She searched the room for some relief from her pain. "What do I do now? I feel awful!" Again she broke into sobs. It was like a weird dream—she was glad she had found out the truth about her mother but felt tormented for the pain she had caused Sarah Buford. "I have my file…I grabbed it from Hector's files just before we left…everything is in it. I wish I had waited until I read all of it."

Ronald dabbed at her tears, "How could you know? It wasn't your fault?" Hoping to find some feminine guidance, he looked at Marissa. "I'm sure she couldn't have taken your calls seriously…what would she have to hide?"

Peterr said, "Everyone has something to hide, Ronald. You, of all people, would know that."

Marissa sat frozen in silence…her thoughts far away from events in this room in Florida.

Peterr turned his attention to Victoria, "A plan… Give Sarah a call and, without explanation, tell her you are sorry…that you incorrectly tagged her with your frustration."

"As if reading from a book, Ronald spoke, I think my family has less to hide than most…the whole world makes up things about my family, most of which are not true." Ronald kissed Victoria on the forehead. "Nineteen years later, Mrs. Manning… Don't you think Victoria deserves to know who her mother and father were?" This time, he glared at Marissa, "Especially, since they are *conveniently* both dead."

Peterr felt defensive but had wanted to know the answers to the almost two decades old secret. "It must have been difficult to carry this around all these years." He held her hand and provided a reassuring smile. "It's okay, Mar. It's okay…"

Marissa collapsed into an overstuffed chair, "It sounds so stupid now, but when she was fifteen it was just what she wanted to do. She was a rich kid, used to getting her way." It was almost as if she had reverted to being fifteen herself. She looked at her fingernails and wiggled her feet. "I'm sorry for the pain I caused you, Victoria…but all my aunt could think of was the shame and consequences to the families." Marissa reached up and grabbed

Peterr's hand. She hesitated, obviously not wanting to go on any longer.

"Please, Marissa…I needed to know." Victoria surprised herself…it was easy to talk to Marissa. "Like Peterr said, 'we all have our secrets,' Mrs. Manning—so it's okay." Again she felt certain warmness as the words lifted from her soul.

Her face flooded with tears, Marissa continued, "Heather was just leaving to go home when Chad showed up. Remember, Charles was Chad's older brother…twenty-three years old and on holiday break from Penn State." She took a deep breath and began ringing her hands. Marissa's voice faded away, "Heather left with Charles and Chad went to a football game…That's where the Bufords thought both of their sons were going. She had no idea she might get pregnant."

"You're saying it was Charles Buford with Heather?" Peterr put his arm around his wife, "Did Chad or Charles know about her pregnancy?"

"No…no one but my aunt. Well, I guess Charles might have known," Marissa sighed, "At least my aunt knew…just before Heather left for Europe."

"So my father, Charles, died skating just before my mother left for Europe? And she died after a horse riding accident." Victoria shot out the words—they had been stuck in her heart as long as she could remember. It was strange, now that she knew, it no longer mattered. It was ironic she had been agonizing over two people who had been dead almost all of her nineteen years.

Marissa raised her head and slowly moved it from side to side, "Yes, he died that winter, right about the middle of February. They said he died at the skating pond…a drowning accident, Victoria." Marissa raised her eyebrows, "Heather had just figured out she was pregnant. There may have been doubts before that time, but now she was sure. His death gave her a way out…you can see that, can't you? She was so frightened she was considering suicide but just couldn't do that to herself or you. She wanted to keep you, but my aunt was a powerful woman, Victoria. She took Heather to Europe just about the same time."

Victoria rushed to her aunt. She could not explain her feelings, she felt compassion, but she also felt grateful to hear of her mother's bravery. "Marissa, I love you, I'm sorry you had to suffer like that." Victoria could not reconcile her feelings with the pain which had been hers over the years—she wondered if her life with Hector Rodrigo would ever be behind her. The real question was not answered, but it didn't seem to matter…she had her mother's best friend…her aunt, Marissa, to console her.

Ronald studied Marissa's face. Her eyes were closed as if soaking in all the love Victoria could pour out. Victoria had Hector's file, but Ronald had the report given to him by his private investigators. His lips tightened as he considered the obvious dilemma.

Chapter 44

As often happens, sudden storms at sea change direction as quickly as a champion quarter horse. Miracle should have been happy the storm had abated, but all he could think about was the safety of his son. The burning question would remain—did he get the message he hoped the MiG had recorded; "How long 'til we reach Kingston?"

The captain snorted and became busy cranking the wheel hard to starboard, but he also did a quick reckoning, "The storm cost us some time, Mr. Smith, maybe we lost an hour…not too bad, considering."

"So about two hours?" Miracle's voce was flavored with a large dose of hope. "Let me try your girl's purple cell phone…please."

Both men chuckled, not just at Miracle's joke, but as much from relief that the storm had moved away to the South East.

In a few minutes, Miracle had confirmed his appointment with the sea plane. His fingers trembled as he punched the numbers to connect him to Ronald's cell. His heart quickened as he heard the sound confirming a connection. The sound of his own voice seemed to vibrate in his ear. "Come on…come on!"

"Hello?"

The single word caught the old man off guard, for a few seconds he felt his throat tighten. "Ronald?"

A torrent of relief flooded out of the receiver, "Father, I have been so worried… I…"

"Did you get my message?" Miracle practically shouted.

For what seemed like a lifetime the phone went silent. "Message…? What message?"

"Where are you now, Ronald?"

"Fort Walton…remember, we were…"

"Get out of there, Ronald…NOW!"

"But I'm waiting for you, here... When will you be here?"

"Son, don't be concerned with me. Get out of there… Get in the MiG and get out of there NOW!"

Ronald was never one to do anything without a good reason, sometimes with laborious explanations required before he even budged—it had been a problem from the first day he could speak. "Why, Father…what's happening?"

"Just get out of there…NOW!" Miracle paused and then spoke only one word, "Susame!"

Ronald was bewildered, he didn't even know why, but he understood what his father was trying to tell him. "Here?"

"Yes, soon…you have to get out of there now. Please, for once in your life do as I tell you." Even Miracle was surprised by the pleading in his voice.

Ronald could not believe his ears. Why would his father do such a thing? "Father…you ordered this?"

"No…not really. It's Barnacle… He's gone crazy! It was supposed to be an energy program. He has even blackmailed the U.S. Government."

"Can't you stop him? Do U. S. authorities know about this?" By now Ronald was shouting into the phone—everyone upstairs rushing to Ronald to see what was the matter.

At the mention of the name, *Barnacle,* Marissa loudly muttered, "My God!"

Both Ronald and Peterr Manning turned to look at her. "You know this name? Marissa?" Peterr cocked his head as he examined her expression.

Ronald spoke softly into the phone while Victoria looked from face to face. "What's going on?" Victoria could tell something life threatening was going on, but she could not understand just what it was.

Suspiciously, Ronald studied Marissa, "What do you know of this name?"

For days she had been trying to tell Peterr about her assignment to link up with the person called, *Barnacle,* now the words came rushing out of her mouth. "It was an… ULTRA TOP SECRET assignment, Peterr. You know how that is, I was not supposed to tell you. Barnacle, I think it's a *he,* plans to test a Susame device. We're not sure how reliable the Intel is but…"

Her voice was frantic, Victoria didn't like the look she saw on Ronald's face, "What's a Susame…device?" To make sure she had his attention, Victoria grabbed his arm.

In a flash Ronald put together his father's warning. The fact they had chosen Florida for the *test* was not that surprising but the thought he might be sitting in the strike zone instantly panicked him. He ignored Victoria, "Father, are they testing in Florida?" He tried to act calm but the tremor in his voice gave him away.

Miracle did not even want to say the words, but he had to, "Yes, Ronald…Fort Walton *is* the target." He let the words sink in, "You must get in your MiG and get out of there…NOW." The old man could feel his heart pounding…he felt helpless. "Clear one hundred miles as quickly as possible, maximum altitude."

"How close are they?" Ronald rolled his eyes at his question.

"They are in a large freighter in the Gulf…international waters." Again, Miracle shouted, "Get out of there!"

"We will, Father…where are you?" Ronald looked at the phone as the tone buzzed, indicating a disconnect. He tried *69 but couldn't get a reconnect. "We got cut off."

Beside herself, Victoria screamed, "WHAT IS A SUSAME …THING?"

Marissa grabbed Victoria by the shoulders, "A big bomb, Victoria." Judging from what she heard of Ronald's phone conversation, she knew they were in trouble…and no time for technical explanations.

Peterr picked up the phone, "We have to notify the base… Marissa, get the kids." Things were happening so fast his mind swirled with questions, "Ronald?"

"Yes, I know what you want to know, Peterr." Ronald grabbed Victoria's hand and made ready to head for the airfield hanger where his MiG was berthed. "The Base is the target for the test…blast range, at least fifty miles. They are now in the Gulf…in a freighter, international waters."

Peterr wondered what was happening, why he had missed it from the beginning. He had been on this project to find out who was behind the device and where the device was being built, but now it wasn't making sense. When he had finished relaying the information to base HQ, he set down the phone and looked at Marissa. "What…why are you still here, Mar? Get the kids."

Her face was blanched, "Hillary Blain said 'They want all of us over at the Colonel's home.' Some men in military outfits have everyone tied up." Too many things were hitting too fast and her face changed into a mask of pain as her mascara began to ooze down her cheeks. She clasped her fingers over her lips and struggled to breathe. "The kids, Peterr…they've got our children."

Ronald and Victoria stopped short of the door, "Your children? They've got your children…who are *they?*"

Victoria asked, "Why?"

Marissa sighed as she took a deep breath, "Chad and Sarah are there, too. I don't know who these men are or even why they have the kids, except…"

"They must want all of us…" Peterr stopped as Marissa grabbed his arm and spoke in his ear. "Remember the bugs at Chad's? Maybe they heard us too."

Peterr nodded, "They want ALL of us—that means you and Victoria too, Ronald." He stepped close to Ronald and Victoria. He whispered, "Our home is bugged…that must mean they are not yet releasing the device if they want us over there."

Years of fending for him made Ronald indifferent to the problems these two strangers were having, but he could see the struggling anguish plain enough in the eyes of Victoria. "Do they plan to kill us?"

"I don't think so…if that were the case; why not just leave us here to fry." Peterr shrugged as he looked at Marissa. "We've got to go."

Ronald hesitated to see Victoria pleading with her eyes, "Let's at least find out what this is all about, Ronald."

"You realize we might not make it out of here alive, Victoria… Father said they are going to use Fort Walton Beach as a test site."

Peterr interrupted, "Look, Ronald…let me call the base and have them prep an aircraft…maybe we can get out of this yet. Or maybe something else is going on."

Ronald tightened his lips, "I have my own plans, Peterr, but I'll go along with you…just for the kids and because Victoria wants me to."

Away from the bug devices in the room, Ronald recounted his thoughts; *I wish I knew the exact whereabouts of Father. Maybe the answers are at the Colonel's house, but then…what was going on that the children were being held hostage?*

"I know what you're thinking, Ronald, and I hope you're not right. Where does the Colonel fit into this whole thing? For my money, I want to know if *Uncle Blainy* is holding the kids for their protection or for some other reason.

Chapter 45

The De Havilland Beaver's Canadian DHC-2 450 hp Pratt and Whitney engine gnawed into the afternoon sky above the harbor at Kingston. The seaplane had been completely restored, one of the best aircrafts ever produced. Miracle Chu sat in one of the twelve seats in the back of the plane, his mind considering his options as he watched the streams of seawater trail off the two sea floats.

Through the loudspeaker, the pilot spoke to Miracle, "Sure you don't want to sit up front?"

The roar of the single engine mixed with the words but he understood the inquiry. Chu shook his head and waved his hand to make sure the pilot knew he had no interest in sitting up front, not that he was afraid, but he needed to think. When he was first approached about the Susame Project he had only seen the potential for energy, climate control, and making a lot of money, he had never considered the massive death and destruction it might create. Now that he was older, he no longer gave money and powers that big a place in his life, certainly not in the last twelve hours—his wife would never have approved of this sort of thing in the first place.

For the fifth time, Miracle touched the rectangular object in his pocket—it reminded him of the small remote he had used to turn on the Christmas tree lights at home. In the tail section of the seaplane was a large box that contained thirty-five pounds and six ounces of C-4 explosive. He constantly wrestled with his intension to detonate the explosive on the freighter, if they would not listen to reason and halt the test. Blackmail was one thing, but killing innocent lives was a totally different thing. There was a good chance he would be unable to escape being on the freighter when the C-4 went off.

"Are you doing all right back there?" the pilot barked over the loudspeaker.

Miracle responded with a smile and a friendly wave and said, "Doing fine…okay." The plan was for him to pull up next to the ship and Miracle would be picked up by a dingy that would ferry him to the freighter. Undoubtedly, he would be welcomed with open arms, as they were expecting a large box full of United States one-hundred dollar bills—a down payment for today's services.

Jolted awake from an unplanned nap, Miracle heard the pilot yell, "I see an old freighter coming up on the starboard side, is that the ship?"

Miracle moved forward and sat in the co-pilot's seat. "Yes, that's it."

"Looks like a real rust bucket, if you don't mind me saying so." The pilot rattled off his thoughts and then shrugged when Miracle did not respond. Next he proceeded to circle the freighter and ascertain there were no dangerous objects floating or hiding just below the surface. "Okay, we're going in…tighten your belt."

As the De Havilland banked sharply to the side, Miracle and the pilot could see the shimmering of the late day water—like a mountain field covered with tiny glistening flowers, points of light dancing about on the tops of gentle waves. It looked so peaceful…who could believe that inside of the hull of the old freighter was a device that could rain death and destruction upon on humans, animals and plants that had been what made up Earth since the dawn of time. With the pressing of a plastic button, one person would yield the same destruction as a massive earthquake, a tidal wave, even thousands of Krakatau volcanoes. The cruelty and indifference of such an act was about to be unleashed on purpose.

"What's this freighter doing out here?" Like the boat captain, normally the pilot did not ask questions, but the old Chinaman seemed like a nice guy…not like some of the drug dealers he sometimes dropped into isolated places.

"Waiting on docking papers in order to deliver a shipment of auto parts used for restoring old 1950s show cars…" Miracle broke a half-smile at the absurdity of his statement. "Could you wait for me…I might not be more than an hour or so…if things go right."

"Okay, but I have to be back to Kingston for tonight…son's birthday, you know." He smiled, "He'll be fifteen." He adjusted his flaps as he continued speaking, "Got a daughter that's five…a kind of surprise." He laughed and gave Miracle a gleeful smile.

"Maybe I should let you go back to Kingston… I can visit with my son and catch a flight tomorrow." The words sounded good and it made him feel good but it wasn't in the cards. Miracle looked at the happy pilot. For the first time he noticed the man's accent and his soft brown skin. The way the father of two young children spoke about his family touched Miracle to the core.

"Are you sure? I can wait…my wife will understand." He knew she would be happy about some extra money, but miffed if he arrived too late.

The man's words were heartfelt—Miracle reached out a hand and gently patted the man on his forearm. "No…you just reminded me how much I need to see my son. You have a good time at the birthday party."

Smoothly, the seaplane touched down, the noise like an aluminum boat slapping against the wake of a passing boat, then settled into its rest upon the sea.

Miracle sighed as he wondered if he would ever see his own son again.

Chapter 46

With the base on alert status, a private crew prepped Ronald's MiG 31. Peterr Manning, Marissa, Ronald and Victoria considered their own options.

"I think we're missing something," the thought hammering itself into Peterr's brain. "Chad and I searched the base looking for a laboratory… We were led to believe there was a group of techs doing research on this…Susame thing." He looked at Marissa, "I then find out that *you* were supposed to be making contact with the guy we believe has orchestrated this whole thing?"

Marissa rolled her eyes and, ignoring Peterr's question, she spoke in crisp words,

"Our children…Peterr. We have to get over to the colonel's house." Opening the door to the garage, she asked, "Do we walk or drive?"

"I want some answers now! What the hell has been going on?" Peterr narrowed his eyes and tilted his head to the side, "Is this why Sarah was hit by that car and you were drinking so much?" He had thought it was because of the research he and Chad Buford had been doing but this was completely unexpected.

It was like watching a tennis match—Ronald and Victoria were forced to swivel their heads from side to side as the couple engaged in verbal bashes.

"May I suggest we take a car, just in case we need to dash for the airport." Ronald wanted to make a point, but he also wanted to get moving—he was never one to wait when he could be *doing something.*

Peterr did not shift his eyes from his spouse, "And what about you pretending to be drunk some of the time…I suppose that was part of your assignment?" Not waiting for an answer, he turned toward Ronald and Victoria. "Good idea…we might need the car. Ladies in the back…please." He shot Marissa one more questioning look.

Smugly, Marissa grumbled, "This is not the time, Peterr…later."

The drive was short, one of the reasons the two couples had used Hillary Blain, the Colonel's daughter, as their babysitter. Hillary had been able to walk to their homes…saving extra car trips. As they pulled up to the front of the home, they were surprised how innocuous the surroundings looked—the lawn was well manicured— shrubs and trees trimmed. Why did it look so peaceful when so many things were manifesting a sense of foreboding?

"Peterr, listen to me— the most important thing is to get the children out of the house and to safety." Marissa spoke calmly, as composed as she could be, but deep down she was gravely aggravated her children were being held hostage. She felt an instinctual urge to tear the perps to shreds. "Let's get in there and take care of this. It's just as likely Uncle Blainy has heard something and is keeping the kids safe." She didn't really believe that.

In a show of agreement, Peterr nodded and reached for the door handle.

Ronald opened his door and stood still—used to the drill of protecting his father. Waiting for something to happen, he glanced around the perimeter…he could see nothing overtly threatening.

"You know, the colonel might be a prisoner as well… Maybe he and Hillary were forced to call us. As unlikely as that is, it's still a possibility." Peterr began walking toward the front door of the colonial style home.

Almost casually, one of the doors to the two-door opening slowly swung open, but no one emerged.

"You two wait here," Marissa counseled to Ronald and Victoria. She tipped her head toward the parked car.

"Are you armed?" Ronald asked, a logical question, but the tone indicated something else.

"You think our lives are in jeopardy?" Marissa said, wrinkling her forehead.

"You don't?" Ronald retorted.

Marissa continued, "We know the Colonel…and Hillary…has watched our children before…even when we were stationed in Washington DC." She looked at Peterr, "We'll be all right."

"He's got a point, Marissa." Peterr shifted his eyes to Ronald, "If anything looks bad…get out of here."

Ronald grabbed Peterr's arm by the shirtsleeve. "This guy is a Colonel…don't you think he knows about the freighter and the Susame test?"

Peterr hesitated and said, "Hell, I don't know, Ronald. probably." In a fit of temper, Peterr pulled free and barked at Marissa, "Let's get the kids."

As Peterr and Marissa Manning walked toward the open door, Victoria jumped into the front seat while Ronald took the driver's spot. "What's bothering you, Ronald?"

"Something's wrong here. My father says there is a powerful device on the freighter…maybe powerful enough to wipe out the entire state of Florida, maybe the whole country…but nobody seems to care." Ronald hesitated, as if trying to put things together. "So either my father is lying, or he is suffering from a mental breakdown… Either way, something's wrong. But, I'm pretty sure he believes, at least, there's truth to the rumor."

"What I don't understand is why those two, Peterr and Marissa, don't seem to be too overly concerned about what the babysitter said… there are some military men in the house…? They're concerned, yes, but not like I would be."

Ronald considered the question, "I really don't know…maybe there are bodyguards or something…but, I don't like it." He opened the door on the driver's side. "I'm going in to see what I can find out."

"Not without me…I'm not staying out here alone." Victoria's eyes were wide, like when she was on the balcony and shot Hector. She could feel her breathing increase as if under water and needing to gasp for air. "Are you armed?"

"Of course…I never go anywhere without two weapons—a shoulder-blade knife and .32 caliber revolver in the small of my back."

Armed or not, Victoria could not see how those could be effective against a couple of real soldiers, but she had an illogical trust in Ronald…she was scared but felt safe with him.

The concrete driveway looked gray, like the face of a dead man or a well aged tomb stone. Along the edges were black driveway lights which came on when it was dark—

they also contained sensor devices announced all activity. Ronald motioned for Victoria to follow him as he walked on the grass side of the driveway—behind the driveway lights.

Approaching the open doorway, they were greeted with another surprise. The door opened wider still and a large man stepped out below the archway. "You are quite welcome, Ronald Chu…and of course your young friend, also. Please come in, we have some things to discuss." The man then turned about and went back into the house.

Ronald hesitated—this was the kind of situation where he would usually consult with his father…why had he not heard from him? Shouldn't he be taking Victoria and speeding away to safety, to let everyone else fend for themselves, but yet he felt himself drawn into the mystery of the situation. "I don't like it, but I'm not sure we have a choice here, Victoria."

She nodded and grabbed his left hand… Hector had taught her to always leave the man's gun hand free. At times like these she wished her ugly memories of the South American pervert would disappear forever. "I just want you to know I love you,

Ronald…I always have. So if we don't make it out of here—"

He had lots of precious words he would like to say to her, but for now all he could say was "I know…"

Together, they moved toward the door and into the house. Whatever was lying ahead, they would face it together—good or bad, life or death.

Chapter 47

The roar of the departing De Havilland faded into the southern sky and Miracle stood at the bottom of the gangway and felt a surge of envy for the life of a simple pilot. The aviator would be sitting down with his family and enjoying his son's fifteenth birthday, unless the Susame beam turned out to be more powerful than predicted. It was times like these he wanted to get his hands on the person who went by the name of Barnacle.

The ship's first mate moved up behind Miracle, "We are most happy to see you, Mr. Chu…and of course a most welcome crate of merchandise." He pointed his chin at the compact box one of the merchant seamen had taken off of the seaplane. "Shall I have it taken below?"

"We had a slight mishap at the loading dock…some of the contents got soaked with seawater. For now, it would be best to put a guard on it and take it to a warm spot in the engine room for drying." Miracle added an apologetic shrug, "We don't want any careless handling and, besides, the sea brine will help to abate some of the newness."

After responding with a knowing bob of his head, the first mate turned to the two men standing behind him, "Take this crate to Locker Four…stay with the crate until you are relieved. No one goes near it!"

"No one is to disturb the box…no one." Miracle added. He watched as the crate disappeared behind a heavy steel door. For the first time, he realized his remote detonator would have to transmit though multiple layers of steel…and the signal might not carry that far. At best, he would have thirty minutes to travel at least fifty miles…not a likely scenario.

"Have we heard from our dear friend, Barnacle?"

Miracle had not heard the ship's captain approaching him and the first mate.

"No…Barnacle has been strangely quiet. Frankly, I'm a bit concerned."

Miracle wrinkled his brow and pursed his lips. "You don't suppose Barnacle has met with, shall I say, foul play?" Nothing would make Miracle happier, but this was no time to display feelings.

"Could be—" The Captain speculated. "We heard about your misfortune in Columbia, but nothing about Barnacle… Was your pilot killed…we all liked him?"

Miracle found it difficult to hold back his emotions, "Yes, he was killed…he was a fine man, a true warrior." Miracle paused and took a deep breath, wanting to talk about the pilot but knew it was only a question—the captain didn't really care. "What's the status on the test?"

"I'm sorry, Mr. Chu, I thought you knew. We are awaiting verification of funds and the 'go-ahead' from Barnacle. I understand you brought aboard a large crate." He tipped his head and waited for Miracle to respond.

"Quite so…the currency is drying out…in one of the rooms." He turned to the first mate, "Correct?"

"Yes, sir, I thought it would be the best place and the most secure," the first mate said, addressing the captain.

Bobbing his head the captain said, "I believe it will dry out just as easily if we take it out of the crate and allow more hot air to circulate around the bills." Without looking at Miracle he added, "Don't you agree, Mr. Chu?"

Chu had not expected this turn of events…he was not used to people questioning his decisions and was both angry and panicked. "If that is what you want to do, Captain, I suggest we place the crate in a vault or in your cabin…but, only after I have had a chance to examine your Susame equipment. After all, Barnacle and I would like to make sure what we are buying, shall I say, the genuine article."

The captain winced. He too was not used to anyone questioning his decisions at sea. "Most reasonable, Mr. Chu…" He turned to the first mate, "Take the crate to my quarters…lock it in my vault. We will go to the tech lab and bring Mr. Chu up to date."

Miracle turned his head and stared off at the distant horizon. He was certain he was going to be trapped on this ancient freighter…would never again lay eyes on Ronald. In chess, the captain's move would be called "mate" but it was not yet "check mate"—Miracle still had a few moves left and fingered the remote detonator in his pocket…perhaps having the C-4 closer to the detonator would turn out to be a good bargaining chip and the thought left him reassured.

"That seems like a reasonable idea, Captain…First Mate, just make sure the security is tight." He touched the captain on the forearm, "One more thing…I think we should wait for Barnacle to arrive. Agreed?"

The captain pushed his eyebrows together and squinted. There was no doubt but what he seemed surprised and now his "authority at sea" was indeed being directed. He responded with words that, this time, carried more weight, "I didn't know Barnacle was scheduled to make an appearance… My understanding is his identity remaining a secret has been what's kept the rascal alive all this time." The freighter captain cast an inquiring eye at Miracle. "Rumor has it you have met with him…is it true?"

The captain began walking toward the nearest access point, a large metal door held open by an oversized iron hook. "We can go to operations and check in with Barnacle." With those words the captain stepped through the open chasm. "I didn't expect you to tell me if you had met with Barnacle, so please excuse… nothing more than an inquiring mind."

Shifting his glance away from the horizon, Miracle followed behind the captain and heard the large metal door close behind him—the small cavern like a primordial mausoleum. "I believe, Captain, you will find this venture important enough for Barnacle to make this exception…quite likely heavily disguised."

The captain made no reply except, "Watch your step." They now began to walk down hill into the "belly of the beast" where the research center and launch control equipment were coordinated.

If only he knew Ronald was safe…but even that was not enough. Miracle had hoped to be able to reap a financial fortune without killing millions, and so, to him, the test was unnecessary—believing the United States Government to be run by a bunch of frightened rabbits. "What's the status again?"

"Now that you are here…we just need to sign off with Barnacle and verify the funds you brought aboard." The captain paused, "Is there a problem? We can activate the test in less than one hour from countdown. Our end of the operation is to open a hole in the magnetic field that protects the earth."

"I see…so you are certain it works," Miracle probed.

"The technicians tell me they are confident…they just don't know the potential extent of possible damage because that's impossible to ascertain in a laboratory setting."

"Oh…" was all Miracle could manage to say.

Chapter 48

Inside the home of LT COL Blain, Ronald and Victoria glanced around the foyer—the Blain household interior was much more opulent than the outside. The white marble floor was crowned by a glistening chandelier which seemed a bit too ornate for even the colonel's tastes. Several guards decorated the perimeter like wax statues dressed in fatigues.

Blain appeared though a double-door entrance to their right. "Do come in and join us, won't you?"

The room smelled of firewood—the sweet odor of hardwood crackling in a Georgian-style setting. An arrangement of four couches filled the center of the room, flanked by large wooden bookcases stuffed with impressive leather-bound volumes. Seated on the couches were Chad and Sarah Buford, Peterr and Marissa Manning and Blain. The colonel motioned for Ronald and Victoria to sit down. "Our time is short, please, have a seat." Gracious words, but still a command.

Ronald sensed tension in the air—there was something wrong here but he was in too deeply to attempt retreat. "What's this all about?" The words just fell from his face, as if uncontrollable but part of destiny.

"Very good, Ronald Chu—I like a man who comes to the point…at least, I think I

do, so I too can make things clear to you."
He paused and leaned back in the leather
couch. "These fine parents realize I am
holding their children—as guests. Your
father is aboard a ship in the Gulf of
Mexico…and of course, Miss Victoria
Rodrigo, or should I say, Buford, you are all
my guests until this whole mess is resolved."
He hesitated and picked up a smoldering
cigar stub occuping a corner of a white glass
ashtray. "At which time we will all forget
what goes on during our little chat."

Neither Victoria nor Ronald made a move
to sit where they were instructed, causing
several of the guards to adjust their weapons
to a *ready* position. Colonel Blain held up
his hand, "I don't think any violence will be
necessary here, do you?" The colonel was
directing things as if the situation were a
'reality show' for TV. His eyes narrowed
into a menacing glare.

Ronald helped Victoria take a seat and he
sat down beside her. "Is this about
Susame?"

"Of course this is about Susame, Mr.
Chu…what else?"

Chad Buford interrupted, "This…man
plans to test the readiness right here in Fort

Walton Beach…more specifically, at the military base." He shifted his look to watch the reaction on the Colonel's face. "Isn't that right, Colonel?"

The room turned silent while everyone waited for the response. The fire crackled, the London–style, grandfather clock ticking back and forth—in the distance, the unmistakable sound of jet aircraft. Slowly, the colonel got up and tossed the cigar butt into the fireplace then he stepped to his large mahogany desk. Like a tired Mongol warrior, he sat down and released a long sigh. "Major, you would never have been brought into this if you had not stumbled onto our, shall I say, little problem with the technicians who decided to desert the project." He raised his hand and pointed at Sarah, "Your wife almost lost her life when one of Hector Rodrigo's people decided to eliminate both of you, but I was sure I could use that *close call* to keep you distracted." He grinned, "You see, that freak accident changed things…and, incidentally, it wasn't Hector's guy that did that."

Sarah started to speak, but Chad nudged her, and she settled for giving him a dirty look and tightening her lips.

"At my suggestion, she bugged your house…did you know that?" The pompous colonel didn't wait for an answer. "Peterr, I'm talking to YOU now… Marissa even put on her drinking routine to explain any unusual actions on her part…pretty clever, I thought." Colonel Blain seemed to be talking to no one in particular as he looked toward the ceiling. "Marissa was charged to make contact with the person known as Barnacle…she did that…with my help, Peterr."

"So you were behind our wild goose chase into the underground tunnels on the base." Chad almost bolted out of his seat but reconsidered the option of doing so and took a look, once again, at the men posted about the room.

You might say, well…what has happened here on this pig's sty base in the humid hellhole called Florida has been in our national interest, Chad…Peterr." Blain leaned over his desk—his arms folded in front of him. "It's all about money…money and power. This Susame thing has managed to loosen up billions of dollars needed to strengthen our countries," Blain searched for the right words, "…military position."

Victoria was shivering, not from cold, but from relapses of her time with Hector Rodrigo. "Hector used to say those same, sickening things, Mr. Colonel, and he was an evil man. With his drugs and killings, he and Ronald's father put lots of money into this...this, Susame thing. It must be evil too...how can you do this thing, Mr. Colonel?"

Blain stood up and ran his fingers over the American flag behind his desk. "I love this flag and all it stands for." He moved from behind his desk and stood at 'parade rest' as if addressing a group of military cadets. "Right now...just outside of our territorial water...in the Gulf of Mexico to be precise, is a large freighter. We have intelligence that says the Susame device will be tested right here...and soon." He raised his voice and loudly shouted, "THAT SHALL NOT HAPPEN ON MY WATCH!"

After adjusting his necktie, he calmly announced. "Very shortly, a strike force from this base will reduce that freighter to a pile of seabed rust." Turning to Ronald he said, "I'm sorry your father is currently on the freighter, but...well, it's just bad timing."

"You're going to kill my father…and you write it off as BAD TIMING?" Ronald felt the blood pounding in his veins—suddenly, his face was red and his eyes bulged with anger. "What sort of insanity is this?" Ronald shrugged, "How do you know he's on the freighter…what would he have to do with this? He would never agree to testing that Susame thing here, on U. S. soil…it would reflect badly on the Chinese government and our family. He was born here!"

At this point, Hillary Blain came through the doors, "How's it going, Father… I heard shouting." She looked at the six *house guests*…quickly turning her head to face her father.

Blain smiled, "Everything's fine, Dear. We'll be through here soon…just see to the children."

Sarah and Marissa were hard pressed to contain themselves—fearing Hillary would leave the room before they had a chance to ask about their children. Almost in unison, they said, "Where are Warren and Betsey? Carl and Glenda?"

Hillary only looked at them.

"The children are asking when *Uncle Blainy* will come up and play with them, Father—" For the first time since the parents had known Hillary, she responded in a cold and military fashion. "I'll tell them you are here and will see them shortly…just as soon as you have concluded our business here." Hillary smiled at her father then sauntered from the room—her bearing indicating she was no longer a babysitter, more a part of her father's minions.

Sarah Buford turned burning eyes toward the indifferent face of Colonel Blain. "You sonofabitch…who do you think you are? You can't hold us here, much less kidnap our children. They'll court martial you for this!" She could tell her words were falling on deaf ears, on a person immune from petty threats. Sarah turned to Chad and mumbled, "Aren't you going to do anything?"

It was evident Sarah's attitude summed up what everyone was thinking, but it was just that…no more than a venting based on fear and frustration. None of them were in a position to do anything.

One thing Chad could count on was the Colonel's concern for his own skin and that of his daughter. As long as the both of them were in the target area, the rest of them would be safe from the Susame's beam—at least he hoped he was right. "Sit down, Sarah…," Chad said. "This is not the time for Picket's Charge. Let's see where the Colonel is going with this."

"The problem is…you do not have all the facts, Sarah. Chad is right…and I would advise you not to make idle threats. As your superior military officer, I do not take such words kindly." Again the colonel paced to the window and looked toward the Gulf of Mexico. "Our nation is in serious trouble and you all are here to attest to that fact. After 9/11 I'm not sure our nation can afford another disaster, especially one that kills millions of innocent citizens. We are also facing serious invasion from our *neighbors* to the south."

"What do you mean? Do you plan to let them attack?" Peterr Manning said. "What about the air strike, do you intend to cancel it?"

"That would not sit well with the public, Colonel," Marissa added, "especially when it is learned you could have prevented it with a preemptive strike."

Ronald Chu took a deep breath. He had been in situations like this before and knew it would not be wise to challenge the person holding the cards. "I know you are aware of my father's influence… He has many friends in Washington. Can I assume you will hold off the air strike until he has left the freighter?"

With the tone of a preacher finishing a brief sermon, the colonel droned his response, "I am afraid, Ronald Chu, your father's death aboard the freighter may very well help some of his friends in Washington to realize even a good man like your father can be duped into supporting the cause of terrorists. That may be an over simplification…but accurate." He turned and faced Ronald, "He will be sorely missed…but I do not see how I can risk holding off our air strike, running the risk they will attack our nation before we can act."

Chapter 49

Miracle expected to find a technical room replete with blinking lights and whirling machines but found instead a deserted locker room—adequate but hushed. "I would have thought you would need more equipment and personnel than what I see here." He shifted his glance from one wall to the other. "Very sparse."

"And my XO (Executive Officer) tells me your crate is very…sparse, Mr. Chu." The freighter's captain tilted his head, similar to a parent inquiring about his son's poor grade in algebra. "You have brought a large supply of explosives aboard my ship…and very little cash, Mr. Chu." He paused, "What am I to make of this?"

This was not the first time Miracle had been scolded by a dangerous person, but for once he was not concerned about preserving his life. "AND I thought we had agreed to wait for Barnacle to join us…the C-4 is just a precaution. I would advise against trying to disable it, as the person who gave it to me is very skilled at creating, shall we say, dangerously lethal triggers against tampering and, besides, I have armed the contents of the crate." He leaned forward, almost touching noses with the captain,

"Surely, you did not expect Barnacle and me to just bring cash to a meeting where we could not be certain *what* we were paying for, or if we would get anything in return except a mugging. The minute the crate was opened…I was aware of it." Miracle looked around the meager surroundings and shrugged. "Show me what I came here to see. and Barnacle will send the cash. I will then contact Barnacle and give *the all clear.*"

In the background Miracle could hear the movement of several men. The next thing Miracle heard was the sound of weapons being armed—the distinctive *click* echoed off the metal bulkheads.

"I'm afraid I cannot allow that, Old Man." The captain squinted as if struggling to find the right word. "Your friend, Barnacle, knows why, but, evidently, he has chosen to keep you…HOW SHALL I SAY, *in the dark."* He pulled a snub-nosed .38 caliber Colt revolver from his pocket. "Now, I guess we will just have to deal with Barnacle for the money…it has all been arranged."

"Then you intend to activate the Susame beam?" Tightly, Miracle gripped the remote detonator in his sweating hand—his fingers felt weak, but steady. "You do not have to do this…thousands will die…maybe millions." Miracle was surprised by the response.

Snickers and chuckles floated through the air—like a small flock of birds clacking as they rushed from somewhere above Miracle, the sounds gradually faded out. "WHAT beam, Mr. Chu?" The captain waved his gun around the room, "Do you see anything here?" He coughed, "No, I don't think you will find any evidence of a 'death ray'…not anywhere on this ship." He laughed, "Does that surprise you?"

"'Surprise' is a word I would reserve for those who are gullible enough to believe the promises of others." Miracle looked at his surroundings and snorted, "If all you cared about was money, you could have gotten rid of me a long time ago…therefore, *Captain,* I believe you must require something else of me."

Slowly, the captain turned his head in a gesture of frustration. "It's time to stop playing games…we want the final pieces, Mr. Chu, and I do mean NOW. If I have to wait any longer…"

Then the real surprise burst forth… It was as if someone had suddenly pulled the strings on a set of puppets as every head moved to look at the ceiling. There was no way to mistake the sound of a flock of F-16 fighters—the roar, deafening and unmistakable as they passed low and in tight formation. Miracle, the captain, and his men all stood frozen, like children hoping the boogieman would not find them. Just as quickly as the sounds had arrived, they smoothly faded out as the aircraft charged toward the western edge of the Gulf of Mexico.

Displaying a smug smile, the captain said, "We are in international waters…there is no need for alarm. I'm sure the fly-boys were just having fun with us. Barnacle has assured us…we are safe." He opened his mouth to continue speaking, but his words were swallowed by the sound of returning jets—they were coming back.

It was Miracle Chu's turn to smile. "You're an idiot, Captain…you threatened the United States Government…did you really think they would just pay you to go away?"

"Give me the other pieces, Mr. Chu! Where are they?" The captain's face turned to an angry snarl as he shoved the barrel of the .38 into the chest of the Chinaman. "It will do you no good to lie…Barnacle has assured us all, you have the final pieces…the plans, the people." He cocked the hammer, "Where are they?"

Miracle looked around at his captors and nodded. *What is he talking about?* He asked himself, but quickly said, "In the bottom of the crate—" *Buy some time now...* "Under the C-4…you'll find plans and a list of names."

Miracle had no idea about any building plans or names. But then, it was never wise to disappoint.

Chapter 50

With the force of an 8.0 on the Richter Scale, the home of Colonel Blain shook on its concrete foundation—windows rattling to the point of cracking, the massive chandelier in the entrance way swaying back and forth, threatening to fall to the floor. Like little toy soldiers, the guards were thrown against the walls and rolled across the floors. Colonel Blain pitched backward against his large desk behind him, his feet pointing in the air as if in slow motion.

Those on the couches were thrown to the floor as if by some invisible, giant hand. A rolling wave of South American floring covering concreate undulated across the floor—resembling a wave of water one might see at the beach. The couches crashed about like clothes in a dryer.

"Get the guns!" Chad shouted as the weapons once held by the soldiers went scooting past Marissa and Peterr Manning.

Ronald had already grabbed one of the assault rifles as he tightened his grip on an unconscious Victoria. She had been struck in the head by a large brass lamp and blood was flowing down her face onto one of the couch cushions.

Chad moved next to Ronald and put a hand under one of Victoria's arms, "Quick…head for the door, our children are upstairs." He sounded frantic. "Peterr, take Marissa and Sarah and head for our cars…we'll get the kids. Here…take Victoria."

Sarah and Marissa wanted to quarrel, as they were justifiably anxious about their children, but they did not argue. Sarah grabbed Victoria's limp arm and told Marissa to grab the other. Together they moved toward the exit taking them to their cars. Ronald and Chad headed upstairs while Peterr finished collecting weapons and disabling others. The room was a mess, resembling a construction area.

"What the hell was that anyway?" Chad mumbled to Ronald as they carefully made their way up the damaged staircase. "An earthquake?"

Not wanting to think of any other possibilities, Ronald mumbled, "Maybe, but probably not the Susame…maybe the air strike!"

"Yeah, I forgot about that."

They made a turn taking them to the open door of Hillary Blain's room. "Kids? Warren…Glenda, Carl, Betsey?" Chad could not see any of the children and his heart began to speed up.

"Under here, Dad…" Warren Buford came scampering out from under one of the bunk beds; a tearful Glenda came out behind

Warren. "Where's Mommy?" Betsey asked as she and Carl came out following Warren.

"She's okay, your mom and dad are waiting downstairs…we have to get out of here." Chad Buford looked around the room, "Where is Hillary?"

"She told us to get under the beds then she left us here, Dad." Warren was tugging at Chad's arm. "Who's he?"

"A friend, we'll talk later…let's go." Chad led the kids toward the doorway. Ronald grabbed the hands of Carl and Betsey, while Chad took Glenda in tow…Warren followed. "We've got to get out of here…fast!"

Dust and plaster, floating and plumating toward the floor, were still falling from the ceilings and the chandelier was covered with white drywall dust—it resembled an upside down Christmas tree coated with fake snow. There was still no movement from the room where the guards had taken them, but at the foot of the stairs, lying under a spread of flowers from a broken vase, was Hillary Blain. A decorative column had fallen on her and broke her leg. Ronald bent down and scooped her up onto his shoulder.

Outside, the anxious mothers and Peterr waited at the automobiles. Power lines were scattered about the ground, some cars were in a roadside ditch, and portions of the roads were cracked—the air force base sirens wailed as never heard before. It seemed the only thing to do was to head for the base.

On the minds of everyone was what exactly had happened. Overshadowing all of the problems was the joy of having the children safe and sound. Victoria was now conscious and her head injury had stopped bleeding. Hillary would have to go to the hospital, but she seemed more concerned about her father than anything else.

Ronald could only speculate what had happened, about his father and the fate of Florida, the southeastern seaboard for that matter. He tried calling but could not even get a responsive signal, and so he feared the worst. This time, maybe…Miracle could not pull off another phenomenon, another one of his escape acts.

Chad nudged Ronald, "Is she all right?" nodding toward Victoria.

Ronald nodded.

As they drove toward the base, everyone was quiet and wondered what was coming next.

* * *

Confusing announcement find the ai waves and TV, but no one was really explaining anything—only speculations.

It did not take long before a series of inquiries were held, with the public purposely not informed, as the findings were considered to be matters of National Security and, therefore, would never be released to the news media.

Whether the Susame Beam Project ever proved operational was not known, only the knowledge that billions of dollars had been spent trying to develop one. Billions more had been paid to buy one on the black-market. The freighter had exploded from within…and it was assumed the Susame detonation had backfired, causing the vessel to be reduced to cinders. Divers were unable or prohibited for disclosing to recover anything helpful to the investigation.

The culprits in the Susame affair were considered to be Barnacle, whom they never found…Hector Rodrigo, now deceased.

Miracle Chu was exonerated for the sake of his son and international relations with the Chinese Government maintained.

LT COL Blain was the hero of the hour and given credit for having thwarted the planned attack from the freighter and doing so without having to use his fighter jets— which, most assuredly, would have caused an international incident between the United States and China. There was talk of the now full-bird Colonel being the *savior of the nation*—and he was being considered as a possible candidate for President of the United States. His daughter, Hillary, occupied her time by visiting schools as a guest speaker.

Ronald was called back to China to take the honored place of his father but, for now, was making it his life's goal to find Barnacle.

Victoria and Ronald made plans for their wedding and her aunt was to be her maid of honor.

One night, while Ronald was occupied at an airport hanger working on his MiG 31 BM, Marissa and Sarah told Victoria the truth about her birth and the events they had kept hidden from the rest of the world.

Ronald had still not told Victoria what was in the report received from his investigators.

Epilog I

As I had done so many other days, I took the elevator to the ninth floor and, as I stepped out and into the hallway, I listened to my leather-sole shoes clacking out an echoing beat on the white tile laid over the concrete floor. I can't recall the weather, but I think it was warm and sunny. Outside the brown metal door to the hospital room, I was hushed by a nurse who took me by the elbow and guided me away from the patient's door.

"He's in there with his wife and her niece," the nurse whispered.

I thought she was going to tell me he only had a short time to live and said, "Is he dying?"

Her head bolted back and she gave me a shocked look, "Heavens no…but I think they have some family issues to settle…something about a boat."

I nodded my understanding—actually, I had wanted to meet some of the family but he had stayed guarded about the whole thing. "I'll just wait over here until they're through." I turned and clacked my way over to a metal chair and sat down. There was nothing to do but wait, so I just glanced about the hallway, but it was not long before the nurse came to fetch me.

"He would like you to come in now." She smiled and led the way to the private room.

After he announced my name to the group, Peterr Manning introduced me to Marissa Manning and Victoria Chu. "I would like you to meet my wife, Marissa Manning…and our daughter, Victoria Chu."

Involuntarily, my head snapped, "What?"

Marissa turned a kindly face to me and said, "The whole thing centers around Charles Buford, Heather DeVunder and, of course, me. It's a long story, but if you have the time I will tell you what really happened that day. You know how men's imaginations can run wild." She gave a nervous laugh.

Peterr attempted to move himself to a sitting position, "Sarah Buford had been living with a ton of guilt about the death of

Chad's brother, Charles. But I think I will let her tell you about that."

"Heather DeVunder found herself pregnant at fifteen, an absolute family disgrace. She considered suicide but instead confronted Charles Buford, Chad's brother. He was to meet with her at the skating pond and offer twenty-five thousand dollars in cash and, of course, the name of an abortionist. He was twenty-three and wanted to avoid any stain on his pedigree." Marissa paused and looked at Peterr. "Not to mention this was not the first time this problem had happened to Charles."

Peterr's hand slid across the bed cover and rested on the top of Marissa's hand. "What happened next triggered everything that followed. When Charles gave Heather the money, Heather threw the bank pouch of money out on the ice. Then she turned and ran away. Charles had on his skates…as Heather left, he rushed after the pouch." After a quick hesitation he continued, "He must not have paid any attention to the warnings about the thin ice…and he fell through the ice and drowned."

"It was an accident…how could she know he would be so careless?" I felt I needed to also interject my understanding of the tragedy. "So where does Victoria come into the picture?"

She went on, "Heather and her mother went to Europe to stay with Heather's uncle on her father's side, Horst DeVunder. The plan was to stay until the baby was born and then return to the states." Marissa rolled her hand and put a death grip on Peterr's arm.

I looked at Victoria who sat quietly and gave Marissa a reassuring smile.

Marissa continued, "After Victoria was born, Heather felt so depressed she went to the bathtub and slit both of her wrists." Marissa took a deep breath. "As the life was draining out of her, she changed her mind. She tried to stand up in the tub but was too weak. She collapsed in the tub and fell, face first onto the plumbing fixtures…it shredded her face and splashed blood and water onto the floor. A real mess—" Marissa looked at Victoria, "After this incident, Heather was given extreme plastic surgery, and Heather DeVunder became Marissa DeVunder."

"So the accident where you and your mythical cousin were thrown from horses was just…made up?" I was surprised at how things started to make sense.

"I saw the birth certificate in Hector's files and the father's last name was Buford…I thought my mother must have been Sarah Buford, so I started giving her those nasty calls." Victoria finished with an apologetic shrug. "The certificate had my hand print and Marissa's…only the certificate said, Heather DeVunder. At first I thought Chad was my father because they abbreviated Charles to Chas, and the writing was in sloppy ink. The 's' could have been a 'd.'"

"My aunt and uncle in Europe had a daughter named Marissa, so it was easy to fake some papers where Marissa had lived and Heather had died." Marissa's face turned sad, "It seems some people will do anything for money or to save the family name."

"So…Marissa is Victoria's mother and you are her stepfather?" I know I sounded a bit confusing the way the words came out but I was definitely uncertain. "Wow!" I reached out a hand to Victoria and she heartily grabbed mine. "Congratulations and congratulations on your marriage."

Victoria blushed and smiled, "You will have to meet Ronald. Mr. Manning, Dad, has told us so much about you."

"Where is Ronald…is he here in the United States?" I heard Peterr cough and looked at him, "Did I say something I shouldn't have said?"

Peterr rattled his head about and looked at Victoria, "Go ahead…tell him."

"Ronald is in Florida… He just returned from China where he learned the identity of Barnacle. Ronald AND MIRACLE are on their way to Washington DC to testify at a Senatorial hearing."

I could not contain my surprise, "What? Miracle is alive?" I almost got whip lash as I looked around. "So they located the culprit, Barnacle?"

"Yes…" she giggled and ignored the second part of my question, "Isn't it a *miracle?"* She giggled again, "Ronald said Miracle knew where his explosives had been stored so when he pressed the detonator he knew he had three minutes to position himself against one of the steel girders, even found a hardhat. He grabbed a wooden workbench and made it to the surface…a fishing boat picked him up and he made his way to a Mexican village.

"Well, I'll be damned…" My face went into a quizzical scrunch, "So what's this about Barnacle…what happened?"

During all the talking, Chad Buford and Sarah had slipped into the back of the room.

Victoria looked at Chad Buford, her uncle, and Chad began talking, "It seems the good Colonel, *the savior of our country,* engineered the whole Susame thing in order to advance what he had hoped to be a Presidential career. He was sure, after he had saved so many people, he would be a shoe-in. Some friends in China confirmed Miracle knew who Barnacle was, that is, that it was good old *Uncle Blainy* and so Miracle and Ronald will be testifying at the hearing."

"You're kidding…I knew from what you said he was a bit of an odd one, but I just thought he had a confused patriotism."

"So did everyone else…they thought he was a super patriot but was actually trying to take over the country. Miracle stopped him from getting his hands on the cash the two of them had stashed in Latin America. They actually set up a sting operation and caught the Colonel red handed." Chad looked around the room as if expecting applause…but all he got was a questioning grin from Sarah.

Epilog II

We talked for several hours and when Chad and Sarah Buford returned I thought it was time to make my exit. But I wanted to hear what Sarah had to say…"Sarah, could you spare a few minutes to tell me why you felt responsible for the death of Charles Buford? It's really a moot point because it wasn't your fault, but I wanted to hear it from you—"

"Yes, of course. Chad knows the story…I finally got up the courage to tell him what happened."

She took my arm and led me out into the hallway and I said, "You don't need to tell me if it will make you uncomfortable, but I must admit I am curious."

"It might sound foolish, but the more I have talked about it the more I feel some relief for my carelessness." Sarah paused, "I was working at the bank when Charles got the twenty-five thousand dollars to give to Mar…Heather, I mean. At lunch I shot off my big mouth and mentioned some things." She took a deep breath, perhaps to calm her nerves. "I didn't know one of the girls at the booth was a previous pregnancy victim of Charles' indiscretions. Can you believe it?"

"Was it common knowledge about the bank?" Knowing how rumors fly around business establishments, it was a logical question for me to ask.

"No, but you see she had been paid off with the same amount—twenty-five thousand dollars. She was furious Charles Buford was going to buy his way out of another pregnancy." Sarah shook her head…her face became troubled. "I had no idea she was one of Charles' victims. She told her boyfriend, and then they planned to confront him at the skating pond." She leaned toward me as if to tell a secret. "You see…Detective Manning, Peterr Manning's father suspected something like this, but he could never prove it."

"So…what happened?"

"The boyfriend decided they should rob Charles, not just confront him…he convinced the girl that Charles owed her more money. Well, Heather did not want to go to the pond just for the money… I got curious so I followed her. She threw the bag on the pond, but I was there just in time to see Charles fighting with the girl from work and her boyfriend."

"Did you tell the police?"

"I tried to but felt so guilty for blabbing things at lunch time." Sarah's eyes went misty, "I saw them push Charles into the thin ice. He just disappeared. The two of them ran into the nearby woods."

"What happened to them?"

"Charles' death was ruled an accident, but the two of them knew I had seen what really happened. Nothing happened until we went to Florida and they were afraid I might tell Marissa what actually took place. They came to Florida, after twenty years, intending to make sure I did not testify against them…they almost killed me. They even made threatening phone calls—" She finally gave me a faint smile. "I turned them in. They will go on trial in Pennsylvania, but it will take a couple of months."

I found it difficult to express my thoughts to Sarah. "You know, Sarah…I sometimes have to laugh at life. Look how strange it is this Susame scare exposed so many secrets and brought all of this together…it was the catalyst that merged the lives of Heather, Marissa, Victoria and you. Without Susame I am not sure you three would have resolved the issues in your lives."

"Perhaps…but I guess we'll never know. Now the trick will be to enjoy what *Susame* has given us."

With that narrative, Sarah Buford got up and shook my hand. I watched as she slowly walked back to the private room of Peterr Manning.

I hummed a happy tune as I again thumped my way back to the elevator. I wondered how many people would ever know the real truth about how the Colonel duped the military and a whole nation.

Years later, I had a chance to talk to Ronald Chu and he left me with some very sobering information. While in China, he had heard rumors that one of their scientists had cracked the secret of the Susame concept. I wondered—*could this be another hoax or, worse yet, true? If true, could the earth, THIS TIME, be destroyed by fire?*

Only God knows.

The end of an absolutely fictional story.

Other stories by Raymond Lee Hegstad

The Blue Fin
The First Manuscript
Chockalet Slueiths (Children's books volumns 1,2,3.
Rescued by Death
Endangerd Witness
Phantom Director's Cut (Salem Grey #1)
Murder Like A Labyrinth (Salem Grey #2)
Ice Cold Murder (Salem Grey #3)

A Killer Vacation

A Magnetic Cataclysm A Sicince fiction romance.

Also found at Amazon and Kindle, Barnes and Noble and other fine book stores Raymond Lee Hegstad

A Magnetic Conspiracy